Awareness
in Healing

Awareness in Healing

LYNN REW, EdD, RN, C., FAAN
Associate Professor
Assistant Dean for Student Affairs
School of Nursing
The University of Texas at Austin
Austin, Texas

Delmar Publishers

An International Thomson Publishing Company

Albany • Bonn • Boston • Cincinnati • Detroit • London
Madrid • Melbourne • Mexico City • New York • Pacific Grove
Paris • San Francisco • Singapore • Tokyo • Toronto • Washington

NOTICE TO THE READER

Cover Design: Spiral Design
Cover Illustration: Kirsten Soderlind

Delmar Staff

Publisher: Diane L. McOscar
Senior Acquisitions Editor: Bill Burgower
Senior Marketing Manager: Hank Bertsch
Assistant Editor: Debra M. Flis
Project Editor: Judith Boyd Nelson
Production Coordinator: Barbara A. Bullock
Art and Design Coordinator: Mary E. Siener
Editorial Assistant: Chrisoula Baikos

COPYRIGHT © 1996
By Delmar Publishers
a division of International Thomson Publishing Inc.

The ITP logo is a trademark under license.

Printed in the United States of America

For more information, contact:

Delmar Publishers
3 Columbia Circle, Box 15015
Albany, New York 12212-5015

International Thomson Publishing Europe
Berkshire House 168-173
High Holborn
London, WC1V 7AA
England

Thomas Nelson Australia
102 Dodds Street
South Melbourne, 3205
Victoria, Australia

Nelson Canada
1120 Birchmont Road
Scarborough, Ontario
Canada, M1K 5G4

International Thomson Editores
Campos Eliseos 385, Piso 7
Col Polanco
11560 Mexico D F Mexico

International Thomson Publishing GmbH
Konigswinterer Strasse 418
53227 Bonn
Germany

International Thomson Publishing Asia
221 Henderson Road
#05-10 Henderson Building
Singapore 0315

International Thomson Publishing—Japan
Hirakawacho Kyowa Building, 3F
2-2-1 Hirakawacho
Chiyoda-ku, Tokyo 102
Japan

1 2 3 4 5 6 7 8 9 10 XXX 01 00 99 98 97 96 95

Library of Congress Cataloging-in-Publication Data

Rew, Lynn
    Awareness in healing / Lynn Rew.
        p. cm. — (Nurse as healer series)
    Includes bibliographical references and index.
    ISBN 0-8273-6397-4 (alk. paper)
    1. Nursing — Psychological aspects.   2. Holistic nursing.
3. Awareness.   4. Nurse and patient.   5. Healing — Psychological
aspects.   I. Title.
    [DNLM: 1.Awareness — physiology — nurses' instruction.   2. Mental
Healing — psychology — nurses' instruction.   BF 320 R45a 1996]
RT86.R49 1996
610.73'01'9 — dc20
DNLM/DLC
for Library of Congress   94–38316
                                                                        CIP

INTRODUCTION TO NURSE AS HEALER SERIES

LYNN KEEGAN, PhD, RN, Series Editor

Associate Professor, School of Nursing,
University of Texas Health Science Center at San Antonio
San Antonio, Texas
and Director of BodyMind Systems, Temple, Texas

To nurse means to care for or to nurture with compassion. Most nurses begin their formal education with this ideal. Many nurses retain this orientation after graduation, and some manage their entire careers under this guiding principle of caring. Many of us, however, tend to forget this ideal in the hectic pace of our professional and personal lives. We may become discouraged and feel a sense of burnout.

Throughout the past decade I have spoken at many conferences with thousands of nurses. Their experience of frustration and failure is quite common. These nurses feel themselves spread as pawns across a health care system too large to control or understand. In part, this may be because they have forgotten their true roles as nurse-healers.

When individuals redirect their personal vision and empower themselves, an entire pattern may begin to change. And so it is now with the nursing profession. Most of us conceptualize nursing as much more than a vocation. We are greater than our individual roles as scientists, specialists, or care deliverers. We currently search for a name to put on our new conception of the empowered nurse. The recently introduced term *nurse-healer* aptly describes the qualities of an increasing number of clinicians, educators, administrators, and nurse practitioners. Today all nurses are awakening to the realization that they have the potential for healing.

It is my feeling that most nurses, when awakened and guided to develop their own healing potential, will function both as nurses and healers. Thus, the concept of nurse as healer is born. When nurses realize they have the ability to evoke others' healing, as well as care for them, a shift of consciousness begins to occur. As individual awareness and changes in skill building occur, a collective understanding of this new concept emerges. This knowledge, along with a shift in attitudes and new kinds of behavior, allows empowered nurses to renew themselves in an expanded role. The Nurse As Healer Series is born out of the belief that nurses are ready to embrace guidance that inspires them in their journeys of empowerment. Each book in the series may stand alone or be used in complementary fashion with other books. I hope and believe that information herein will strengthen you both personally and professionally, and provide you with the help and confidence to embark upon the path of nurse-healer.

Titles in the Nurse As Healer Series:

Healing Touch: A Resource for Health Care Professionals

Healing Life's Crises: A Guide for Nurses

The Nurse's Meditative Journal

Healing Nutrition

Healing the Dying

Awareness in Healing

Creative Imagery in Nursing

D E D I C A T I O N

This book is dedicated with great love and respect to the members of the Championship Support Group: *Judy and John; Lou and Glenn; Sandy and Bob; Dee and Val; Paul and Ann; and to its founder and captain, dick.*

C O N T E N T S

P R E F A C E

In recent years, the discipline of nursing has systematically examined the role it plays in promoting the health of the world's peoples. Nurse educators, researchers, and practitioners have initiated a wide variety of interventions to assist their clients with the process of healing. However, as yet, we have not formalized or integrated our body of knowledge about the factors that promote or that interfere with healing. Interventions that primarily teach the client or the client's family about disease and the medical treatment for the disease have long been part of nursing practice. These interventions target the cognitive level of awareness in human beings because nurses believe that knowledge facilitates the healing process. Such interventions evolved from the discipline's knowledge base that was primarily biophysical and psychosocial in nature.

At present, the majority of nursing textbooks address the cognitive level of awareness for nurses and their clients. That is, they organize what is known and can be known about the biophysical and psychosocial dimensions of human beings through the rational mind and ordinary consciousness. Few books, however, address concepts of other levels of awareness such as the intuitive and the transcendent. Books about holistic nursing provide a comprehensive view of healing that begins to shed light on these other levels of awareness. What is still missing in nursing literature is a book that focuses primarily on multiple types of awareness within the nurse and within the nursing client that promote optimum healing. The purpose of this book is to fill that gap.

The primary focus of this book is the concept of awareness as it relates (a) to the nurse's use of diverse ways of knowing in organizing and synthesizing nursing knowledge to use in helping nursing clients to heal themselves and (b) to the nursing client's use of diverse ways of knowing about self and one's place in the universe to facilitate healing.

The book is organized into nine chapters followed by an annotated bibliography and indexes. The chapters move from a generalized overview of the major concepts, assumptions, and theories of awareness in the healing process, through a presentation of specific barriers to awareness and healing, and then to a series of exercises that facilitate awareness in both nursing clients and nurse-healers. Each chapter is designed to communicate with the reader on the three levels of awareness described herein. Each chapter begins with a quotation selected because of its inspirational, illustrative, or instructive characteristics. Each quotation is followed by a vignette constructed from true case files that have been altered to protect the identities of client and nurse without destroying the essence of their healing interactions. Each vignette is followed by an exploration of related concepts and theories that help to explain and validate the theme of the vignette. After reading each chapter, the reader is invited to reflect on her personal types of awareness.

Chapter 1 introduces the conceptual framework including the basic concepts of awareness and healing as they are used to guide materials presented in subsequent chapters. Theories of awareness are presented briefly. Healing as an expanding phenomenon of concern to nursing is also presented briefly and current research on body listening and Therapeutic Touch is introduced. The conceptual framework represents a multidimensional view of human consciousness that is central to the process of healing through human interactions.

Chapter 2 provides a philosophical foundation for healing and the relationship of this process to the complexity of expanding the awareness of both the nursing client and the nurse-healer. This chapter incorporates many expressions of philosophies expressed by nurse theorists and clinicians. The focus in this chapter is on various worldviews or philosophies that have influenced and benefited nursing as it has developed. The chapter does not espouse one particular set of assumptions as *the* philosophy of nursing; rather, it suggests a synthesis of views that provides the unique perspective for healing in nursing practice.

Chapter 3 introduces the many factors that hinder the healing process by interfering with the development of awareness. These barriers include anxiety, the fast pace of living on schedules, distraction within the environment, overstimulation from the environment, and defenses against pain and sorrow. These barriers exist in both the nursing client and the nurse-healer. Examples illustrate the effects of these barriers on both nursing client and nurse-healer.

In chapter 4, the concept of aesthetics and its relationship to a healing environment is presented. Much of the content focuses on sensory experience and how management of the environment contributes to the process of healing.

Chapter 5 begins with identifying the personal knowledge of the nurse-healer and the nursing client. Personal knowledge is knowing not just *about* oneself but actually knowing *the self.* Such personal awareness is essential to an authentic encounter with another person. This authentic encounter is often the impetus for healing or the actual process that signals that healing is taking place. Personal knowledge is based on possibilities rather than limitations and is developed through an intuitive process of bringing diverse bits of information and experience into a coherent whole.

Chapter 6 addresses the process of synthesis of knowledge and experience by both nurse-healers and nursing clients. Nurse-healers have knowledge about the complexity of human life and the process of healing. This knowledge comes from diverse patterns of learning and understanding phenomena about themselves and about their clients. Similarly, nursing clients experience the complexity of life and learn to understand themselves through healing processes. Knowledge (cognitive storage of information in the brain and memory of emotion-filled situations) and experience must be synthesized to develop the wisdom that anticipates and is essential to healing.

The aim of chapter 7 is creative nursing interventions that facilitate healing by increasing the awareness of nursing client and nurse-healer. The emphasis is on using diverse patterns of knowledge and imagination to create possibilities and the implications of these possibilities to the healing of persons.

Chapter 8 begins with a vignette that further illustrates the three dimensions of awareness presented originally in the conceptual framework of chapter 1. The vignette is then analyzed in some detail to demonstrate the nurse's skill in acknowledging the three dimensions of awareness in the healing that occurred in a long-term relationship with a client. This chapter is designed to bring the myriad ideas presented throughout the book into sharper focus before presenting practical exercises to enhance awareness.

The final chapter, chapter 9, contains practical exercises to enhance the reader's personal awareness. These exercises cover a wide variety of activities such as writing, drawing, movement, and visualization. While these exercises will facilitate awareness in the nurse-healer, they may also be modified for use as interventions with nursing clients.

The book concludes with an annotated bibliography of theoretical and research literature to support the content of the book and to be used as suggestions for further study. The book also contains a list of references used at the end of each chapter, additional suggested reading, an index of terms, and an index of authors cited.

Author's Note: In an effort to accurately depict the demographics of today's nurses, most of the nurses in this text are portrayed as women.

A C K N O W L E D G M E N T S

Writing this book was an invigorating and delightful experience. It gave me the time to reflect on many of the wonderful people who were my clients during the 25 years of my nursing career. It also made me reflect on the handful of expert nurses in practice and education who provided me with role models to emulate. It was a pleasure to be invited by Lynn Keegan to write for this series of books on healing in nursing and I wish to express here my heartfelt gratitude to her for her faith in me and her support in editing the final product.

I especially want to acknowledge the contribution of Margaret F. (Ricki) Hudson, an associate professor of adult and gerontology nursing at the University of North Carolina, Chapel Hill, for her thorough review and excellent suggestions for the first draft of this book. Her assistance in bringing my ideas into sharper focus was invaluable and I thank her for the time and care she put into her review.

I also want to express my appreciation to the editorial staff of Delmar Publishers. Bill Burgower and Debra Flis were wonderful with their support and guidance.

Finally, I want to acknowledge the strong support of my family because they believed in me and have demonstrated to me in many ways how healing of disease, injury, pain, and disharmony is possible through very special relationships. My daughter, Carina Limond, is a Registered Nurse practicing in Minnesota. Although she has at times given me credit for inspiring her to enter the nursing profession, I must give her credit for encouraging me to stay with it. Through her examples of tough caring and clear vision in standing up for her ethical beliefs, I feel inspired that her nursing clients, and those of other nurses like her, are in precious hands. Her example was extremely encouraging to me as I struggled to put this book together. My son, Richard, and my husband, dick, have also played extremely important parts in supporting me in this endeavor. Although they are not nurses, they have benefited many times from nursing care and they have done much to assist me in completing this project. As a family, we are diverse and individually self-directed. Yet together we have met the challenges of living and healing through our relationships. Without the experiences of being a wife and mother, I would have known far less about awareness in healing.

1

DIMENSIONS OF AWARENESS IN THE HEALING PROCESS

The doctor's function is to determine by scientific study what particular germ is at work and how to get an antitoxin for it. . . . But it is the nurse who has to be with the patient when he is thoroughly sick, who has to watch and study the development of the disease, the processes that are going on, the stages and phases of the difficulty. All this she has to watch and interpret to a very great extent.

J. F. Forbes, 1919

Sally and Clara

Sally, an attractive young woman in her early 30s, sat in the chair opposite the nurse. She was dressed in loose-fitting slacks and an oversized shirt. Her blond hair hung limply around her face and she wore no makeup. The nurse, Clara, asked Sally why she had made the appointment with her. Sally replied that she did not know but that her surgeon had suggested the nurse might be able to help her.

Sally added that she wasn't sure she needed help; in fact, Sally said, "I'm really not sure of much anymore."

In the 3 months since the surgery to remove a malignant melanoma from her left leg, Sally found herself losing interest in many of the routine activities of her daily life. She took little interest in what or when she ate, how she looked, or where she was going. She had stopped her hobbies of running and swimming and was barely able to provide minimal care for her two young sons.

Sally responded slowly to each of the questions posed by her nurse. Her face showed little emotion or expression and her eyes glazed over from time to time during her first meeting with Clara. In her role as nurse educator and counselor with a medical group, Clara found herself wondering what trauma Sally had experienced and how it was interfering with the healing process following this surgery. Clara pondered how willing Sally might be to embark on a journey that could take her out of the hazy cocoon where she was currently suspended and into the bright arena of awareness and subsequent healing. How much courage and support would Sally need to recognize the depth and breadth of a wound that kept her from living her life fully? How much inner strength and commitment could Sally muster to bring all of her senses into the process of transforming a symbolic wound that was far more serious and meaningful than the bumpy, gray scar on her leg?

For 15 months, Sally and Clara met weekly to struggle with these and many other questions. Gradually, Sally and Clara addressed the reality of the sexual abuse Sally had survived at the hands of her father. Gradually, Sally learned that she was not being punished for being cute or sexy and that the melanoma was not the punishment she deserved for being unable to stop her father's sexual advances. Through the 15 months of talking, crying, drawing, and writing, Sally and Clara became aware of the many complex levels of disease and healing. As her awareness of the many dimensions of life increased,

Sally's wounds healed and Clara developed a deeper understanding
and respect for the power of human life, love, and healing.

Sally's story is unique in the sense that the particulars of
Sally's life that contributed to her illness and the relationship she
formed with Clara happened at a specific time and place in history. The meanings Sally constructed to make sense of the events
of her life were her unique creations. Yet, Sally's story is not
unique in the sense that each human being experiences unto-
ward events and each is the victim of situations beyond personal
control. Each individual creates meanings that connect these
experiences to form a sense of identity and purpose in life. When
awareness of meanings, connections, identity, and purpose is present, the individual perceives a harmony of self with the environment as a whole. But when awareness is limited by lack of
knowledge, perception, and meaningful connection with others,
the individual experiences a disharmony that manifests itself in illness, disease, pain, and discomfort. Healing that accompanies
awareness is needed to restore such harmony.

AWARENESS

The concept of awareness is well-known to nurses and nursing
clients alike, but the term often has a different meaning to each
based on experiences and beliefs. The word *awareness* is derived
from the Old English *gewaer*, which meant watchful (*Webster's
Encyclopedic Unabridged Dictionary of the English Language,*
1989). In modern English, awareness generally means to be
informed, cognizant, and alert about some subject or event.

Nursing students and practicing clinicians know well that
they must be knowledgeable and alert to their clients and the
constantly changing environments in which they practice their
craft. Much of the practice of nursing is based on planned, pur
poseful watchfulness and interpretation of one's observations. The
practice of nursing that seemed to come naturally to women
and mothers, in particular, is now based on an increasingly more

scientifically sound base of knowledge. Indeed, the discipline of nursing contains a broad wealth of knowledge about which the competent nurse must be cognizant. Similarly, the environments in which nurses practice in the closing years of the 20th century are very complex and require a constant alertness to the condition of nursing clients as they interact with these complex environments. Healing, as a process that is never fully complete, encompasses an ongoing awareness of one's body-mind-soul. Those who would facilitate the healing process in others must attend to awareness of body-mind-soul in themselves as well as in their clients.

Nursing clients also must be informed, cognizant, and alert. Being healthy and engaging in health-promoting lifestyles requires that persons gather much information about what facilitates and what hinders their well-being and longevity. Health in a technologically advanced society doesn't "come naturally" anymore; people have to learn and be alert to changes in the knowledge about what helps and what hurts. Recent research supports the notion that informed persons maintain healthier lifestyles than those who are less aware of what promotes health and well-being (Lierman, Young, Powell-Cope, Georgiadou, & Benoliel, 1994).

To recognize a need for healing in one's life, a person must first recognize the disharmony and discomfort that exists. This recognition is what is meant here by awareness. Awareness of one's disharmony with the universe occurs in three different dimensions: the cognitive, the intuitive, and the transcendent. Such multidimensional awareness is not merely the rational knowledge of facts about the physical world. Cognitive awareness includes consciously knowing facts and processing the constant flow of information coming in through the senses.

Intuitive awareness includes other ways of knowing and may be felt directly rather than being known only through the logical, linear, and rational methods characteristic of cognitive awareness. An intuitive flash of the truth about a situation is an example of this kind of awareness. It often leaves the person who experiences it with a sense of mystery or confusion because it is difficult, if not impossible, to put this kind of awareness into words that other people can understand completely. Such direct knowing that constitutes intuitive awareness is very personal and often poorly understood by others.

Transcendent awareness is even less well-understood and is evident in experiences of empathy and nonverbal communication between people. Similar to the intuitive, transcendent awareness is not bound by time or matter. It is the exchange of energy that occurs without rational thinking and analyzing. It is sudden and, therefore, similar to intuitive awareness, yet it permits the closest and most intimate communication between beings. It is the type of awareness that may result from prayer or meditation and encompasses the spiritual dimension of persons and their relationship to the universe as a whole.

Figure 1.1 depicts these three dimensions of awareness. Each dimension is illustrated as variations in concreteness. The figure shows the dimensions of awareness as separate from the person, but it is meant to imply that awareness takes place

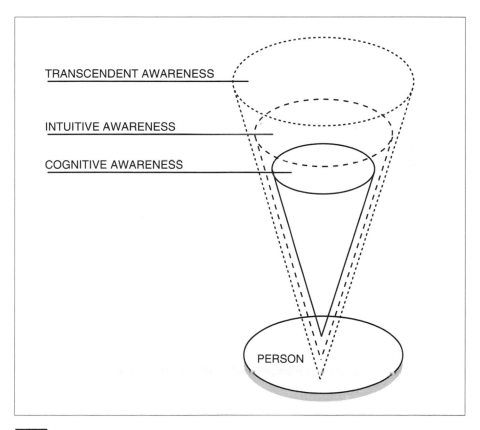

TRANSCENDENT AWARENESS

INTUITIVE AWARENESS

COGNITIVE AWARENESS

PERSON

FIGURE 1.1   Dimensions of awareness in healing

within the context of the person within a larger environment of the universe. Cognitive awareness is portrayed as a solid circle to represent the concrete nature of human cognition. Cognition is both the process and product of knowing. Intuitive awareness is portrayed as a broken circle to represent this more abstract dimension of human consciousness. Intuition is also both a process and product of knowing that is characterized by its sudden appearance in one's consciousness. Intuition is highly personal and subjective and difficult for another person to validate. Transcendent awareness is portrayed as a dotted circle to represent the most abstract and least concrete dimension of human consciousness. Transcendence is also both a process and a product that exceeds the usual experience of waking consciousness. It represents the spiritual dimension of human consciousness which is often neglected in human development because it defies description and direct apprehension.

Each of these three types of awareness is important in the healing process. Each one is crucial to the healer as well as to the healed. In this book, these types of awareness will be illustrated through vignettes that represent actual interactions between nurses and their clients. Maximum healing is possible when all types of awareness take place in both the healer and the healed. Healing is a dynamic and reciprocal process that is constantly going on within and between people. Nursing is one of the disciplines sanctioned by society to facilitate this ongoing process. Nursing continues to evolve with an expanding body of scientific and factual knowledge of how people fit into the environment of the earth and the universe at large. Nurses must be aware of the current state of scientific knowledge about the physical and material characteristics of life to facilitate the healing of their clients. Awareness of their own physical characteristics and possibilities contributes to nurses' ability to understand their clients.

Nurses must also acknowledge their intuitive awareness. Nursing clients cannot always verbalize their problems, their symptoms of disease, or their experiences of suffering. For instance, the infant who is struggling to breathe because of insufficient lung strength or capacity cannot tell his mother or nurse where it hurts or how his body feels. Similarly, the adolescent who sustains a head injury in an automobile accident cannot speak of the pain and discomfort in her legs and spine. Yet, in these and many other situations, nurses intuit or know directly something of the suffering and disharmony of those entrusted to their care.

In nursing, as in other walks of life, transcendent awareness is inadequately recognized. Hospice nurses and those who work in labor and delivery settings are among the few who can verbalize the spiritual connections they feel with their clients and how this awareness contributes to healing activities. Because this type of awareness defies direct observation and description, it is poorly understood and often ignored in nursing education and practice. Thomas (1989) describes a nursing intervention for persons with hypertension that includes the spiritual dimension of both client and nurse. She includes the search for meaning and acting from a peaceful center as hallmarks of spiritual development and notes that integrating these types of awareness into living and working is important for the health of nurses and their clients. Hover-Kramer (1989) states that the attitude that accompanies awareness of the spiritual and transcendent dimension of human experience allows us as nurses to rise above our fears and limitations.

In the example of Clara and Sally, each entered the relationship as nurse and nursing client respectively with limited awareness. That is, each brought with her knowledge of health, suffering, and help. At the beginning of their 15-month formal relationship, each knew very little of the other but both were alert to the need for change. Clara brought with her knowledge of human development and behavior. As she began her initial interview with Sally, she was aware that Sally was a young adult whose developmental stage was one in which intimate relationships and work-related achievements were of paramount importance. However, Sally's behaviors indicated an incongruity between what she was capable of doing and what was actually going on in her life. Mentally, Clara made a note of this incongruity and realized that this was something to remain alert to as she continued to talk and work with Sally. Sally, on the other hand, may not have had the formal knowledge of her developmental stage that would help her understand why her inability to care for her two young sons at this time in her life was part of why she was suffering. One of the tasks to be completed in the nurse-client relationship would be for Clara to help Sally become aware of this aspect of her suffering so that she might correct it if possible or become more comfortable with it through self-understanding and self-acceptance.

While Clara, the nurse, had well-developed skills in observing and interpreting another person's overt and covert behaviors, Sally, the nursing client, probably had less well-developed skills in observing and interpreting her own verbal and nonverbal behaviors. The challenge within their relationship was for Clara to teach and encourage Sally to learn the skill of self-observation and interpretation. This she would do in various ways by helping Sally to become more aware.

Development of Awareness

As human beings grow and develop into more mature beings, awareness generally increases. The infant is an example par excellence of the human being's capacity to become aware of the environment. Ever curious and attentive, infants gradually take in information and become cognizant of the direct and subtle cues from the persons and objects around them. As new knowledge and skills are gained, children expand their awareness of the outer world of things and events. Simultaneously, children become increasingly aware of an inner world of self-concept and personal experience. The children and then the adolescents learn who they are on a psychological level through inward journeys of self-discovery, and what their places are in the world through exploration of the self in relationships. Both avenues to expanded consciousness or awareness have been conceptualized and studied from the perspectives of a variety of disciplines.

Robert Ornstein (1991), president of the Institute for the Study of Human Knowledge, traces the evolutionary process of how humans think. In his synthesis of the many theories and research findings about awareness and consciousness, the mind and the brain, Ornstein claims that human consciousness is evolving from basic instincts of survival to higher realms of spiritual perception. This higher consciousness is a view of reality where each individual is part of a larger, unified organization. He adds that self-observation allows humans to change their minds, to call forth perceptions that are of higher conscious development. According to Ornstein, "humanity has grown in size, strength, and dominion but not in consciousness" (p. 277).

The call to raising human consciousness for healing within the universe can and should be taken seriously by the discipline of nursing. Nursing has a rich heritage of bringing knowledge from other disciplines into the healing environment where nurse and client interact. This heritage provides a base on which to expand the several dimensions of human awareness for healing.

Theories of Awareness

Several theories of awareness are found in the disciplines of psychology, education, and counseling. The conceptualizations that follow represent a variety of approaches to this phenomenon and are meant to provide only a brief overview of this concept. The reader is directed to the primary sources for more in-depth understanding of awareness within these theories. As a discipline that synthesizes knowledge and information from a variety of other fields, nursing benefits from exposure to various views of phenomena such as awareness.

Psychodynamic Theory The classical psychodynamic theory of Freud contains a topographical conceptualization of three levels of awareness, or consciousness (Strachey, 1962). These levels of awareness, or consciousness, influence one's behavior and are identified as the preconscious level, the conscious level, and the unconscious level. The preconscious level of awareness contains information or memory that is not readily available but that can be recalled with some effort. In the case of Sally, everything that had happened to her in the 3 months following her surgery was stored in her memory, but for some reason she had difficulty recalling these details. These experiences could be remembered with encouragement and deliberate effort, but they were not at her immediate level of conscious awareness.

The conscious level of awareness includes that information and knowledge over which the individual has conscious control. For example, knowing that it was spring and likely to be warm when she first visited Clara, Sally was aware that she should dress in cotton clothing rather than bundling up in her woolens. Furthermore, she was aware that dressing this way would help her be comfortable as she faced a situation about which she was confused and in many other ways uncomfortable.

The unconscious level of awareness, according to this classical theory, includes mental functions that are very difficult and, in some cases, impossible to recall. Memories of infant states, including the motivations and behaviors associated with being dependent and self-centered, remain in the individual's psyche. They are, however, incompatible with learned values about adult functioning and, in Freud's view, create anxiety that must be controlled through defense mechanisms such as repression. These motivations seek expression and often manifest themselves through the individual's dreams, impulsive behaviors, and slips of the tongue. In extreme cases, such motivations are expressed through symptoms of psychosis.

Gestalt Psychology   The Gestalt school of psychology developed out of the philosophy and work of artists and scientists in the field of education. According to a phenomenological perspective, this discipline was based on the assumption that the "whole determines the parts," rather than the "whole is equal to the sum of the parts." The German word *Gestalt* has no exact English translation but refers to the structure and context of a whole. The formation of a gestalt occurs in awareness. By focusing on either the figure or the ground in a picture, one is finally able to see the whole. Based on his work with brain-injured soldiers under the direction of Professor Kurt Goldstein, Frederick (Fritz) S. Perls began to develop the theory of focusing on awareness as a way of taking responsibility for one's problems and their solutions (Perls, Hefferline, & Goodman, 1951). Gestalt therapy was designed to help healthy people grow and develop their unique potentials. Most therapy is conducted in groups and focuses on the individual's development of awareness. In particular, Gestalt therapy emphasizes the importance of awareness of the existential moment, or how the individual experiences life in the here and now. Gestalt therapy also emphasizes the importance of the individual developing awareness about those neglected or underdeveloped components of oneself. Through integrating these awarenesses and taking responsibility for one's thoughts, feelings, and behaviors, the individual becomes more fully developed and capable.

According to Gestalt theorists, personality evolves in three phases. These three phases are the social, psychophysical, and spiritual and are all present at birth. These phases represent potential dimensions of awareness. The social phase is evident as the infant begins to show an awareness of other people, particularly the parents. The psychophysical dimension focuses on the individual's awareness of being a person. This phase includes development of the self-concept and body image. The third dimension emphasizes an awareness that goes beyond the physical self and relationships with others to a more intuitive, transcendent, or spiritual awareness of one's place in a larger whole.

Stevens (1971), a Gestalt therapist, describes three zones of awareness: awareness of the outside world, awareness of the inside world, and awareness of fantasy activity. Awareness of the outside world includes sensory experience such as seeing, hearing, tasting, smelling, and touching. Awareness of the inside world includes sensory experience with inner events of the person such as feeling muscular tensions and twitches, itchy skin, and the pressure of one's shoe on the great toe. Awareness of fantasy activity includes imagining, guessing, thinking, remembering, and anticipating.

The Gestalt therapy and Human Potential Movements enjoyed great popularity through the 1960s and into the 1980s, but they were not without their critics. As Edwin Schur put it in 1986, for persons to continue to explore their feelings and their bodily sensations is an invitation to self-absorption and egocentrism. He added that increasing an individual's self-awareness would not help with problems of a social nature that go beyond personal or interpersonal levels.

Client-Centered Therapy   The client-centered approach to psychotherapy was created and advanced most notably by Carl Rogers (1951, 1961). A basic assumption of this approach is that the individual has the potential or capacity to be competent. In other words, human beings are motivated toward self-actualization. Three essential components of this approach to helping and healing are genuine caring or empathy of the helper, congruence between the helper's inner experience and outer expression of this experience in the relationship with the person being helped, and unconditional positive regard for this person. Awareness or consciousness within such a relationship is a symbolic representation of experience. When an individual is free from defensive anxiety about an experience, that individual can freely and symbolically express that experience accurately. However, when an individual is highly anxious about an experience, the anxiety distorts the symbolic expression of the experience. The experience is less available to the individual's awareness when anxiety is at a high level. In the healing relationship, the client is helped to express a congruence between inner experiences (awareness of feelings, thoughts, and memories) and outer behaviors (appropriateness of decisions and actions). Such an individual's self-concept symbolizes a congruent awareness of all personal experiences.

Rogers asserts that when an individual is not aware of the fullness of personal experience, that person does not act in the most constructive way possible. In contrast, the human potential is actualized through increasing awareness of all of one's experiences. A human being who is aware of internally constructed thoughts and feelings can thus be aware of the demands of society and act in a responsible and productive manner.

Psychosynthesis   Another branch of psychotherapy, known as psychosynthesis, also includes the concept of awareness as a grounding technique (Assagioli, 1971). This means that simply becoming more aware of our motivations and connections between thoughts, feelings, and behaviors is not sufficient for lasting psychological change or growth. Rather, the individual learns to *ground* new awarenesses so that pain or depression do not result from feeling overloaded or overwhelmed by new information and knowledge about oneself. New awarenesses are grounded when they are moved from the realm of ideas or fantasy into the realm of daily living. Insights are taken from the abstract and placed into the practical arena of daily activities. New ways of thinking, acting, and feeling are practiced in real-life situations rather than merely enjoyed during a guided fantasy exercise. Psychosynthesis has been found useful in the health professions by encouraging clients to become aware of choices and increasing responsibility for growth, health, and fulfillment in life.

Therapeutic Hypnosis   Recent research increases our understanding about the mind-body-soul relationships and how we view the processes that were once associated with the mind, the body, and the soul as separate entities as aspects of the whole.

Rossi (1986), in a book entitled *The Psychobiology of Mind-Body Healing*, discusses therapeutic hypnosis as a method to facilitate the wholeness of the human being by increasing awareness of how one processes information and how information can be misinterpreted and stored in the body. Hypnosis is conceptualized as transforming an idea into an act. Through hypnosis an individual can become more aware of how misinterpretation of words and events can lead to illness and how obtaining new and unexpected awareness can promote the healing process.

Many fascinating accounts of mind-body healing that have occurred through therapeutic hypnosis are found in Rossi and Cheek's (1988) book, *Mind-Body Therapy: Ideodynamic Healing in Hypnosis*. These examples point to the importance of communication networks within the body. The discovery of neuropeptides, which are characterized as informational substances, helps to explain why the body responds in a negative way to the literal interpretation of words and how awareness of the intended message is associated with healing. Opiate receptors located throughout the body form a network of communication. These receptors alternate between energy and information states and may also help to explain why certain healers are able to alter energy patterns through touch or acupuncture to facilitate healing in the body.

Stress and Coping   The pioneering work of Hans Selye (1956) in the process he called the *General Adaptation Syndrome* led to the development of programs of stress management. Much research has come out of this conceptualization of how the biochemistry of the body responds to situations experienced within the psyche and in the social environment. Events in themselves may be referred to as stressors yet they carry various degrees of eustress (good stress) or distress (harmful stress) for a particular individual. The meaning of a situation, the appraisal of a stressor as a challenge or a threat, is crucial to the biochemical response of the individual's body to that situation.

Learning adaptive coping strategies begins with becoming aware of those factors that are stressful. Through attention to those experiences and responses that are harmful, one can begin to control stressors so that the response is one that promotes, rather than hinders, health. Although many situations and circumstances are beyond the control of the individual, how one thinks and feels about that experience is amenable to personal control. Anticipating the outcomes by looking at a situation as a threat is very different from anticipating outcomes from the same situation seen as a challenge. In the former, the individual believes that personal resources are insufficient to meet the demands of the situation whereas in the latter, the individual believes that such resources are available and sufficient.

Educational Theory   Donald A. Schön (1987), in his book entitled *Educating the Reflective Practitioner,* coined the term *knowing-in-action* to reflect the spontaneous and tacit knowledge that people exhibit in a variety of situations. He uses the example of knowing how to catch a ball. This knowledge is dynamic rather than static and begins with anticipation and awareness of the ball coming toward us. The final act of catching the ball is the product of a continuous process of anticipating the movement of the ball relative to the awareness of the placement and adjustment of one's hands. He adds that this process of anticipation, awareness, and adjustment is necessary to call one's activities intelligent. Consequently, when people learn to perform a specific activity, they are able to act without having to think about each step.

HEALING

The concept of healing is essential to understanding the nurse-client relationship. Nurse theorists at the University of Minnesota have identified the focus of nursing as *"caring in the human health experience"* (Newman, Simes, & Corcoran-Perry, 1991, p. 3, italics in the original). Although this statement of nursing's focus does not include the word *healing*, the human *health experience* includes this phenomenon. The word *healing* is derived from the word *hale*, which means whole. As will be seen in subsequent chapters, nurses care for others with the purpose of contributing to their wholeness. In the example of Sally, the lack of healing of her physical wound was related to a deeper lack of healing of her integrity as a developing adolescent. Because Sally was unaware of the part the sexually abusive experiences played in her approach to social situations, as well as the part the attitude she took toward her body played, she could not understand at first the many factors that contributed to her illness as well as the healing process.

Clara understood that healing could take place within a genuine encounter between nurse and client. Both nurse and client are simultaneously vulnerable and strengthened through the authentic encounter between them. Both the client's and the nurse's awareness are part of a larger whole connecting them. Through this unique and conscious relationship, healing that is primarily intended for the client also benefits the nurse. The relationship offers a vehicle for mutual expansion of awareness and simultaneous healing.

Healing in Nursing

In *The Nurse as Healer*, Lynn Keegan (1994) provides a historical overview of healers and healing practices from various cultures. In this book, Keegan also identifies various types of healing, including the metaphysical, spiritual, and the physical. She describes nurses as healers who begin with self-healing. Particular skills that nurses use in healing relationships with others include guiding others to discover new choices for health-promoting behaviors, modeling self-care behaviors, listening actively, and sharing insights with clients without imposing personal beliefs and values.

Many conceptual models of nursing published between 1960 and 1980 focus on the interaction between nurse and nursing client. Although the term *healing* is used infrequently, the interaction between professional and client is emphasized as an essential ingredient in assessing the needs and resources of the client and in designing and implementing nursing therapeutics. Nursing theorists whose works may be consulted for a more detailed understanding of such interactions include Orlando (1961, 1972), Wiedenbach (1963), King (1981), Travelbee (1971), and Paterson and Zderad (1976). For example, Orlando states that nursing has been characterized historically as an immediate responsiveness of one individual to the suffering of another. *To nurse* meant to promote the growth and devleopment of another through an interpersonal process. Similarly, Paterson and Zderad

(1976) emphasize the primacy of the nurse-client relationship. Based on an existential approach to human interaction, these nursing theorists describe the encounter between nurse and client as one of intimacy and mutuality. Although they do not use the term *healing* in their phenomenological theory, Paterson and Zderad focus on the dialogue between nurse and client that leads to more well-being for both.

Recently, Martha Price (1993), a nursing faculty member of the School of Nursing at the University of Washington, developed a theory of body listening. This theory is based on a phenomeno-logical study of how healthy and chronically ill adults understand the experiences of their bodies. Participants in this study were nine healthy men and women and nine chronically ill persons who had asthma and multiple sclerosis. All of these participants described body awareness that directed much of their behavior and provided meaning for many of their physical experiences. Similarly, they all described energy as awareness of circadian rhythms, requirements for sleep, and individual limits. Price further explicates the body paradigm that she conceptualizes as each person's perceptions of physical capabilities, limited availability of energy, what can be under the person's control, and what is normal for the person. She discusses how this theory is clinically significant because it offers the nurse a range of possibilities for helping the client with health restoration and maintenance.

Nursing has addressed healing over time from an empirical or biomedical perspective. That is, nursing has developed much knowledge about physical wound healing. The most apparent example of this is the number of publications and research studies done on the best way to facilitate the healing of decubitus ulcers. Similarly, from the growth and development perspective, nurses have long been involved in the healing rates that are associated with age and the environmental influences on the healing of physical wounds and injuries.

A few nurse practitioners and researchers have focused on the relationship between their own consciousness awareness and outcomes of healing. Based on Martha Rogers's (1970) conceptualization of persons as irreducible and multidimensional energy fields in constant interaction with the environment, Therapeutic Touch (TT) as a healing intervention exemplifies this relationship. Nurses who practice TT consciously choose to focus their awareness on the intent to heal. In so doing, they engage in healing meditations that influence the energy system of the client. This type of intervention is based on the assumption that there is an interconnection between everything in the universe, including the nurse and the nursing client.

The research of Janet Quinn, a nurse, and Anthony Strelkauskas, a microbiologist, shows that the TT intervention has a positive effect on the functioning of the nursing client's immune system (Quinn & Strelkauskas, 1993). They based their study on Rogers's (1970) theory of persons as multidimensional energy fields in constant interaction with the environment and assumed that nurses who practiced TT would intentionally intervene to repattern the energy fields of their clients. They took both physiological (lymphocytes in blood) and psychological (anxiety and affect balance) measures of nurses and clients before and following TT. Results were that both the nurses and their clients experienced decreases in anxiety levels, increases in positive affect (i.e., joy, vigor, affection, and contentment), and positive changes in immunological composition. The future will undoubtedly see more nurse researchers join with members of other scientific disciplines to unravel some of the mysteries of the nurse-client relationship that contribute to healing in both nurse and client.

References

Assagioli, R. (1971). *Psychosynthesis.* New York: Viking Press.

Forbes, J. F. (1919). Psychology for nurses. *American Journal of Nursing, 19,* 423–427.

Hover-Kramer, D. (1989). Creating a context for self-healing: The transpersonal perspective. *Holistic Nursing Practice, 3* (3), 27–34.

Keegan, L. (1994). *The nurse as healer.* Albany, NY: Delmar Publishers Inc.

King, I. M. (1981). *A theory for nursing: Systems, concepts, process.* New York: John Wiley & Sons.

Lierman, L. M., Young, H. M., Powell-Cope, G., Georgiadou, F., & Benoliel, J. Q. (1994). Effects of education and support on breast self-examination in older women. *Nursing Research, 43,* 158–163.

Newman, M. A., Simes, A. M., & Corcoran-Perry, S. A. (1991). The focus of the discipline of nursing. *Advances in Nursing Science, 14* (1), 1–6.

Orlando, I. J. (1961). *The dynamic nurse-patient relationship.* New York: G. P. Putnam's Sons.

Orlando, I. J. (1972). *The discipline and teaching of nursing process.* New York: G. P. Putnam's Sons.

Ornstein, R. (1991). *The evolution of consciousness.* New York: Simon & Schuster.

Paterson, J. G., & Zderad, L. T. (1976). *Humanistic nursing.* New York: John Wiley & Sons.

Perls, F., Hefferline, R. F., & Goodman, P. (1951). *Gestalt therapy.* New York: Dell Publishing Company.

Price, M. J. (1993). Exploration of body listening: Health and physical self-awareness in chronic illness. *Advances in Nursing Science, 15* (4), 37–52.

Quinn, J. F., & Strelkauskas, A. J. (1993). Psychoimmunologic effects of Therapeutic Touch on practitioners and recently bereaved recipients: A pilot study. *Advances in Nursing Science, 15* (4), 13–26.

Rogers, C. R. (1951). *Client-centered therapy.* Boston: Houghton Mifflin.

Rogers, C. R. (1961). *On becoming a person.* Boston: Houghton Mifflin.

Rogers, M. E. (1970). *An introduction to the theoretical basis of nursing.* Philadelphia: F. A. Davis Company.

Rossi, E. L. (1986). *The psychobiology of mind-body healing.* New York: W. W. Norton & Company, Inc.

Rossi, E. L., & Cheek, D. B. (1988). *Mind-body therapy: Ideodynamic healing in hypnosis.* New York: W. W. Norton & Company, Inc.

Schön, Donald A. (1987). *Educating the reflective practitioner.* San Francisco: Jossey-Bass Publishers.

Schur, E. (1986). *The awareness trap: Self-absorption instead of social change.* New York: Quadrangle/The New York Times Book Co.

Selye, H. (1956). *The stress of life.* New York: McGraw-Hill.

Stevens, J. O. (1971). *Awareness: Exploring, experimenting, experiencing.* Lafayette, CA: Real People Press.

Strachey, J. (1962). *Sigmund Freud: The ego and the id.* New York: W. W. Norton & Company.

Thomas, S. A. (1989). Spirituality: An essential dimension in the treatment of hypertension. *Holistic Nursing Practice, 3* (3), 47–55.

Travelbee, J. (1971). *Interpersonal aspects of nursing* (2nd ed.). Philadelphia: F. A. Davis.

Webster's encyclopedic unabridged dictionary of the English language. (1989). New York: Crown Publishers, Inc.

Wiedenbach, E. (1963). The helping art of nursing. *American Journal of Nursing, 63* (11), 54–57.

Suggested Reading

Burkhardt, M. A. (1989). Spirituality: An analysis of the concept. *Holistic Nursing Practice, 3* (3), 69–77.

Rew, L. (1989). Intuition: Nursing knowledge and the spiritual dimension of persons. *Holistic Nursing Practice, 3* (3), 56–68.

Stuart, E. M., Deckro, J. P., & Mandle, C. L. (1989). Spirituality in health and healing: A clinical program. *Holistic Nursing Practice, 3* (3), 35–46.

2

NURSING'S ECLECTIC WORLDVIEW AND IDEAS OF HEALING

Caring as the human act of being expresses in definable and sometimes elusive ways the mystery of being human.

Sr. M. Simone Roach, 1987

Joshua and Cheryl

Joshua was 11 years old when he first went to summer camp. Just 2 short years before, he had undergone an emergency tracheotomy following an episode of respiratory failure. Joshua had been living with asthma since he was 4. Although Joshua looked as healthy and energetic as any other preadolescent boy upon arrival at the camp, his mother was very apprehensive about leaving him out in the woods several miles from the nearest hospital with a hundred other children with various types and degrees of asthma. Although it had been operating for only 3 summers, Joshua's mother knew that the camp had already established a remarkable reputation. She had heard that the medical and nursing staff were very caring and knowledge-able. As she helped Joshua check into camp, her anxiety began to drop as Cheryl, one of the many camp nurses, began to talk about the purpose of the camp and the kinds of activities Joshua could experience during the week ahead.

Cheryl emphasized that although the majority of children attend-ing camp had the medical diagnosis of asthma, several of the staff's children were also attending and a philosophy of self-responsibility and health promotion would be encouraged among all the campers and staff alike. Cheryl told Joshua's mother about her belief that chil-dren were valued and that they were capable of learning to take care of themselves. Further, she explained that the camp gave the children a significant opportunity to work and play with children and adults who would not treat them as different or sick because they had twitchy airways. In this social setting, the children could learn to rec-ognize their strengths and limitations, and demonstrate responsibility for taking their medications and treatments, while supporting other campers to do the same.

This example of Joshua, his mother, and the nurse, Cheryl, shows how healing is based on a philosophy or worldview. It is clear that Joshua has a physical condition or disease that may interfere with his full participation in many of the usual activities of childhood. His history of asthma and the lifesaving tracheotomy provide a context in which people around him, such as members of his family and classmates at school, will express certain beliefs that include their expectations for his behavior. Many of these beliefs and expectations could influence Joshua negatively. He could develop feelings of being different, of not belonging, and of general disharmony in his world. If he is con-sistently treated as if he were sick or in need of extraordinary protection, he could begin to believe that he is incapable of lead-ing a full and satisfying life. Cheryl expresses her philosophy that Joshua should be allowed to experience the same kind of fun activities associated with camping that other children who don't have asthma enjoy. She believes that by permitting him to have this kind of experience he will be prevented from becoming stigmatized by society and labeled by his disease. She shares with Joshua's mother some of the assumptions that nurses make about children with chronic illnesses. Cheryl explains that these children have value and identity apart from their medical diagnoses, that they have the potential to learn and develop as responsible individuals, and that they are part of an important social network that embraces wholeness and harmony in the world.

In this chapter, many of the philosophical beliefs that have influenced nursing theorists and clinicians are presented. Because beliefs and values modify behavior, those who practice nursing and healing will benefit from exploring where ideas such as caring, healing, and awareness originate.

NURSING'S PHILOSOPHICAL UNDERPINNINGS

The discipline of nursing has matured and evolved over hundreds of years. Because of this process of maturation and evolution, the philosophical underpinnings have also undergone maturation and evolutionary change. Nursing has been shaped and reshaped through dynamic visions that have been altered by the way human beings have adapted in response to their ever-changing environments. Human beings are the central concern of the nursing discipline. Their capacity for wholeness and living in harmony with their environment further distinguishes nursing's unique concern about human beings and their potentials for health and well-being. Although there is general agreement about the major phenomena of concern to nursing, several extant philosophies of science have traditionally influenced the knowledge base that informs nursing practice.

The purpose of identifying the philosophical frameworks fundamental to a discipline is to state the explicit assumptions, values, and beliefs upon which models or theories for practice are based. A philosophical framework or worldview provides boundaries for the model or theory, and from it one can establish guidelines or principles against which a practice model or theory can be examined and/or evaluated. A philosophy of nursing identifies the values and beliefs held by members of the profession and functions as the basis for action by nurses toward their clients. The goal of a philosophy of nursing is the pursuit of understanding the truth about the discipline and its phenomena of concern.

In the mid-1800s, Florence Nightingale began to formalize the education and training of nurses. Nightingale envisioned nursing as an art. She believed that womanly virtue and duty along with meticulous training in sanitary knowledge would produce a skillful nurse. She further asserted that nursing was an art by which one could "put the patient in the best condition for nature to act upon him" (Nightingale, 1946, p. 75). She believed that no science existed that could cure the patient; only nature cures. This worldview was the basis for her *Notes on Nursing*. In her *Notes on Nursing*, Nightingale further clarified her beliefs that nursing was more than mere administration of medications and treatments prescribed by medical doctors. She emphasized the importance of working with the environment to ensure patients had adequate fresh air, sunlight, nutrition, control of noise, and cleanliness. She also expressed a strong commitment to empowering patients to do things for themselves and to involve them in planning care activities. Nightingale's beliefs and values influenced nurses to develop their own cognitive awareness of how the environment contributes to healing. Many of these ideas have formed the basis for further philosophical and scientific exploration as the nursing discipline has evolved over time.

Since the time when Florence Nightingale first wrote about her beliefs about healing and about how nurses could contribute to these beliefs, members of the nursing discipline have developed a number of conceptual models that focus on the relationship between nurse and client. Other models focus on the needs of nursing clients, while still others focus on the activities of nurses, which are known as nursing therapeutics or interventions. The published literature in nursing over the past century and a half reflects a variety of philosophical views. These views contain beliefs and values about human beings, their environments, and the state of health or process of healing. Beliefs and values often exist deep within human beings and contribute to attitudes and behaviors that are apparent to self and others. However, such beliefs and values are sometimes not apparent to oneself, and it is this lack of awareness that hinders self-healing or one's ability to facilitate the healing of others.

While nursing has been criticized, and has criticized itself recently for lacking a unified philosophy, it may be that an eclectic approach to selecting the best ideas represented by a variety of philosophical views is actually a strength because it allows for the inclusion of many ideas that may be useful to the discipline. Furthermore, the uniqueness of the nursing discipline may also rest with its ability to tolerate, synthesize, and celebrate a variety of perspectives. As shown in chapter 1, nurses in practice continuously confront complex situations that call for a high tolerance for ambiguity and uncertainty; thus, eclectic philosophies may facilitate comfort in such complex situations. On the other hand, the limitations of individuals choosing freely from many worldviews include the following:

1. There is a lack of a common language about the assumptions on which the knowledge base and practice of the discipline are built

2. There is a lack of mutual trust between nursing practitioners and scholars and scientists

3. There is a lack of agreement about the phenomena of concern to the discipline

4. There is a lack of a unified direction for further development of the discipline

This chapter focuses on nursing's worldviews as they relate to healing. It does not espouse one particular set of assumptions as *the* philosophy of nursing. Rather, it suggests a variety of worldviews that provide the framework for healing in nursing practice. Several major philosophies have formed the frameworks for many nursing conceptual models and theories: empiricism, positivism, existentialism, historicism, holism, idealism, and phenomenology. Philosophies of science have strongly influenced the discipline of nursing's approach to its science while other philosophies have had a direct influence on the art of nursing practice.

PHILOSOPHY

Philosophy is the study and interpretation of ideas and experience. It is a search for truth and/or reality. As a formal discipline, philosophy is divided into four major branches: metaphysics (which includes teleology and ontology), epistemology, logic, and ethics. Teleology refers to the purposes, goals, and values found in the universe in general, while ontology refers to the basic beliefs of a discipline and deals with reality in an abstract sense. Epistemology is the branch of philosophy that deals with how we can know truth or reality. Logic addresses questions of how we reason or make inferences about reality, and ethics answers questions of how we ought to or should respond to reality.

Philosophy for and of Nursing

Barbara Sarter, an American nurse philosopher, notes that there is a distinction between "philosophy *for* a discipline and the philosophy *of* a discipline" (1988, p. 5, italics in original). She states that a philosophy *for* a discipline such as nursing means that nursing makes use of the ideas put forth by the discipline of philosophy to facilitate the work of nursing. For example, philosophies of science identify the assumptions and methods used to establish a discipline as a science with a circumscribed body of knowledge unique to that discipline. Nursing has used the philosophy *of* science *for* nursing. In contrast, the philosophy *of* a discipline arises out of the thinking of that discipline itself. Conceptual models and theories extant in nursing literature reflect the use of philosophy for the development of nursing knowledge or science. However, there is increasing evidence that nursing is capable of producing its own philosophy, which identifies the unique worldview or perspective of nurses themselves. This chapter provides an overview of several of the major philosophies that have been used *for* nursing as well as the unique ideas that reflect philosophies *of* nursing itself.

Empiricism, Reductionism, and Logical Positivism   Empiricism has its roots in the doctrine that truth comes from actual observation and experience. The meaning of words, for example, can be under-

stood only if they are connected with the experiences of those using the words. Truth is thus justified by experience. Francis Bacon (1561–1626) believed that truth about nature was derived from observing and inductively making inferences. Bacon's method was to facilitate human beings in the proper use of the senses to establish laws about the natural world. He rejected deductive reasoning as a source of knowledge. Empiricist philosophy was further developed by John Locke (1632–1704) who held the belief that all knowledge comes from the senses or from reflective awareness on how one's own mind works. In contemporary philosophy, Bertrand Russell (1872–1970) clarified the principle of verification and contributed to the school of ideas known as logical positivism. Moreover, a group of people known as the Vienna Circle organized themselves in the 1930s and further refined this philosophy. Their doctrine asserted that the physical sciences are basic, value-free, theory is either true or false, the language of theory must be formalized, and knowledge can be built only by using the scientific method (Feigl, 1973).

Positivism is the philosophical approach that values the scientific method. Subjects are reduced to precise empirical observations, propositions or hypotheses, and experimental manipulation. This perspective emphasizes observation and experience and began with the flourishing of industry in England in the mid-1800s. The fields of astronomy, biology, and chemistry thrived on this philosophy, and Darwin's theory of natural selection and evolution was an outgrowth of it as well (Kauffman, 1993). The language of empirical science is formal logic and from such formalized language, laws are discovered.

Positivism influenced the formal development of nursing as a professional discipline because it was the prevailing philosophy of science during Nightingale's time and on into the early 1900s. Explicit assumptions that the environment could either interfere with or contribute to natural healing were based on positivism. However, Nightingale also expressed assumptions that did not flow directly out of this philosophical framework. Implicit in Nightingale's *Notes on Nursing* is the idea that healing is a natural phenomenon. One person does not directly act as a causal agent of healing with a direct response in another person. Instead, one person, such as a nurse, who takes on the role of "healer" intentionally provides assistance to an ill or injured person who, under other circumstances, would not need assistance in negotiating and maintaining a healthy relationship with the environment or universe.

There are many examples of healing as a natural, albeit seemingly miraculous, phenomenon. Children who are just learning to walk frequently fall or run into objects, scraping a knee, chin, or elbow. With no application of medicine, such scrapes tend to heal by themselves within a few days. Since discovery of the germ theory, it is now well-known that certain factors support, while others interfere with, this natural healing process. Cleaning the wound with warm, soapy water utilizes principles of both mechanical and chemical asepsis to rid the wounded area of microorganisms that could lead to infection or cause other diseases. Similarly, application of heat to the wounded area brings a fresh blood supply that facilitates the body's natural defense against infection. Covering the wound with a light dressing also protects the wound from further assault and with physical rest of the part of the body contributes to the natural healing process.

Also implicit in Nightingale's view that only nature cures is the idea that the nurse provides healing assistance only to the extent that the ill or injured other person is unable to do these things for himself. This idea may be viewed as a basic ethic in nursing science because it is implied that taking care of oneself is good. This notion is underscored by Virginia Henderson (1966) who wrote that the purpose of nursing is to aid another individual who does not have sufficient strength, knowledge, or will to care for self. Such assistance was to be provided by the nurse only until the person was sufficiently able to once again take care of the self. This value of self-care was further developed by such theorists as Dorothea Orem (1985) and countless nurse researchers in the past three decades (e.g., Allan, 1988; Clinton, Denyes, Goodwin, & Koto, 1977; Rew, 1990).

The research base of nursing knowledge that began formally with the publication of the journal *Nursing Research* in 1952 focused more on empirical observations of biological processes and technological skills employed by the nurses than on healing interactions. This approach reflected a belief in logical positivism and greatly influenced the problems addressed by nursing science and the development of methods to address those problems. More current philosophies of science have gradually influenced the development of nursing science, but the influence of positivism remains.

Today there are many criticisms of the logical positivist view of nursing science. Nursing adopted a biomedical model during the earliest stages of development as a distinct discipline for at least two reasons. First, nursing worked closely with the medical profession and thus the discipline was influenced by basic sciences that described the anatomy and physiology of the human being and theories such as those of the germ that explained many of the phenomena witnessed in clinical practice. Second, those in the nursing profession who pioneered the development of nursing science were often educated in disciplines outside nursing and, thus, were influenced by the dominant view of science, which valued logical positivism as the only credible route to building nursing science. Positivistic philosophy remains a powerful influence on nursing research in which the focus is the structure and function of the human body.

Existentialism and Humanism   Existentialism purports to study *what is* rather than the *why* of things. This philosophical approach emphasizes that human beings exist in a state of becoming rather than in a fixed state. Existential philosophers include Soren Kierkegaard, Martin Heidegger, Jean-Paul Sartre, Martin Buber, Frederick Nietzsche, and Teilhard de Chardin, all of whom have been explicitly identified as influencing the nursing conceptual models and theories of Paterson and Zderad (1988) and Jean Watson (1988). Central to this philosophy is the belief that a human being's existence comes before her essence, which places value on the individual and subjectivity as the starting points of truth. The classic work of Buber, *I and Thou*, emphasizes the value of authentic interpersonal relationships (1970). Buber claims that a person can only become an *I* rather than an *it* through this type of authentic relationship with another person. This philosophy has great appeal to nursing and has been liberally referenced in the recent developments in nursing ethics.

In 1970, Martha Rogers published her *Theoretical Basis of Nursing*, which was to become a classic conceptual model of the nursing discipline. In this introductory text, Rogers discusses the necessity for nursing to view the wholeness of life and the person in *his* entirety (her original works refer to *man* rather than human being). She asserts that the process of life consists in dynamic events of great complexity. Human beings are characterized by their capacity for conscious awareness of themselves and their world. She identifies five major assumptions upon which her theory of nursing is based. These assumptions are as follows (the word *man* in the original has been changed to *human being* to reflect Rogers's and nursing's use of inclusive language):

1. A human being "is a unified whole possessing his own integrity and manifesting characteristics that are more than and different from the sum of his parts" (p. 47)

2. The human being "and environment are continuously exchanging matter and energy with one another" (p. 54)

3. "The life process evolves irreversibly and unidirectionally along the space-time continuum" (p. 59)

4. "Pattern and organization identify [the human being] and reflect his innovative wholeness" (p. 65)

5. The human being "is characterized by the capacity for abstraction and imagery, language, and thought, sensation and emotion" (p. 73)

These assumptions reflect Rogers's beliefs that human beings have value because they exist. She cites existentialism and humanism as espousing those values that are useful for nursing. Although she refers to nursing as an empirical science, she clearly asserts that a mechanistic view of the human being is inaccurate and inappropriate for nursing's commitment to human health. Her views also reflect a belief in holism, although she does not directly name holistic doctrine or philosophy in her work.

The philosophical perspective, or worldview, of Jean Watson provides the foundation for her nursing theory of caring. She includes several themes from the historical nursing literature. These themes are the value of a human being as an integrated self that is greater than the sum of her parts, and the importance of human relationships between persons (including that of nurse and nursing client) and their environments as these relationships affect health and healing. Watson emphasizes her theory as a component of a human science based upon a philosophy that embraces human freedom, choice, and responsibility, holism, aesthetics, and empiricism. It is an open philosophy. This nursing perspective is experiential and subjective, contextual, and emancipatory. Watson credits Teilhard de Chardin, an existential philosopher, with her ideas about love and caring as universal givens (Watson, 1988).

Watson identifies human care as an intersubjective human process and a moral ideal for nursing. She states that the value of caring is found in the self-transcending creative nurse. The necessary and sufficient conditions for caring to occur are knowledge and awareness about the need for care, an intention to act, actions based on knowledge, and a positive change that results from caring. Moreover, she lists 11 assumptions related to human care values in nursing, some of which are paraphrased from other existential philosophers such as de Chardin. These assumptions are that care and love are the most universal cosmic forces and comprise the primal and universal psychic energy. The needs for care and love are often neglected and must be nourished for humanity to evolve.

Nursing's ability to sustain its caring ideal will affect the development of civilization and contribute to the further development of society. Nursing must begin by treating itself with care and love before those who comprise the discipline can treat others with gentleness and dignity. Athough it has received little attention in the health care delivery system, caring is the most central and unifying concept in the discipline of nursing. Medical technology has threatened the human caring role of nursing and the preservation and further development of caring is of great significance to nursing. Human care is seen through interpersonal relationships in which persons identify with one another and reflect their intersubjective humanity. The social, moral, and scientific contributions of nursing to society rest with the commitment to human care values in theory, practice, and research.

As Watson notes in these assumptions, nursing has historically been aware of the needs of human beings for love and care. She adds that the profession must be aware of its own needs with respect to these two concepts and treat the members of the discipline in this way. Her focus is on the interpersonal aspects of caring as the perspective most central to and agreed upon by members of the nursing discipline.

Phenomenology   Closely related to existentialism is phenomenology, a philosophy of science that focuses on investigation of
the meaning and consciousness of the lived experiences
of human beings (Husserl, 1962). Edmund Husserl (1859–1939) is
credited with founding the phenomenological movement. The
object of study is the subjective experience of those individuals
who know the phenomenon through their living processes. In
recent years, this philosophy has greatly influenced many nurse
researchers who seek to understand the meaning of health
experiences in clients rather than to predict objective outcomes
of disease processes or nursing interventions. Ideas that are inherent in phenomenology include an integral view of the world
where all of life and processes are interconnected and have
meaning, and that there are multiple modes of awareness.
Through a process of engagement with the phenomenon of interest, the researcher elaborates a type of interpretive philosophy by
turning to the nature or the essence of the experience. The
researcher uses the self as the primary instrument for data col-
lection and generates those data intentionally.

Martin Heidegger is also considered an existentialist-
phenomenologist whose philosophy has influenced many nurse
theorists and researchers. His work, *On Time and Being*, provides
a foundation for understanding human awareness (Heidegger,
1972). This ontology is appropriate for nursing because
Heidegger argues that being aware is the nature of the human
being. This awareness is of self and other. Because human beings
are self-aware and are concerned with their being in the world,
they can also be concerned for others, which, of course, is essential to caring and to nursing.

An excellent example of how phenomenology guides nursing research is illustrated in a study by Janet Rose, a nurse
researcher and educator from Canada. Rose conducted a study of
nine women who participated in intensive interviews to describe
what inner strength meant to each of them (1990). This philosophy and method were appropriate for this study because the
researcher sought to understand the meaning of the experiences
of inner strength in a variety of women. Rose found nine essential themes from the meanings provided by the women who participated in the study: quintessencing, centering, quiescencing,
apprehending intrication, introspecting, using humor, interrelating,

having capacity, and embracing vulnerability. Rose emphasizes that the nine themes must be considered as a whole rather than as isolated phenomena. Quintessencing is identified as the groundwork on which these women built their inner strength and represents the process of becoming one's best or most perfect embodiment of self. Included in this theme are processes of recognizing, becoming, accepting, and being. Recognizing is the process of being aware of how various life experiences shaped the individual's sense of self and becoming is a process of being aware of how difficult it is to be authentic. Accepting themselves was described by these research participants as awareness of the values and beliefs that were right for them, while the theme of being had to do with knowing their true inner natures. Centering is a theme that refers to the process of both focusing and balancing the external events of one's life with one's inner experiences while being aware of what is central to oneself and what is not.

The theme of quiescencing refers to seeking and being quiet; it means being aware of an inner wisdom where one is safe to retreat and become re-energized. Apprehending intrication is an awareness of knowing and understanding how complicated one's life is and finding meaning in how difficult situations contribute to the development of inner strength. Participants in this research described gaining awareness of their psychological processes through introspection. This includes noticing patterns and recurring themes of responses to life's situations which increase one's self-knowledge. Using humor was an important component of inner strength to many of the women who participated in Rose's study who were aware of this as a key to their growth and self-understanding. Interrelating is a process of reciprocal intimacy with other people and having capacity is the ability to solve problems, face pain, and heal. The final theme, embracing vulnerability, is the process of being aware of one's limitations, weaknesses, and imperfections and using them as opportunities for further growth and development.

Rose's research provides a basis for understanding an important phenomenon in the mental health of women. Awareness of the themes that contribute to inner strength has implications for nurses and other health providers who contribute to the healing of others. For example, from the themes identified by the participants in Rose's research, the practicing nurse could assist women in exploring dimensions of themselves such as their vulnerabilities, centering abilities, and senses of humor. This exploration could lead to a fuller understanding of each woman's strength and capacity for healing. The theme of quiescencing suggests that promoting a quiet and contemplative awareness of one's inner resources of wisdom and strength may aid in the healing process. Similarly, gaining awareness through introspection of the patterns and intricacies of one's life provides the individual with another resource to promote the healing process.

Paterson and Zderad first published their book entitled *Humanistic Nursing* in 1976 and based much of it on their work in psychiatric settings. They begin the book by explicitly stating that nursing is an experience lived between human beings. They draw on existential and humanistic philosophy in which they assert their beliefs in human awareness and authenticity. They were heavily influenced by the philosophy of Buber and the *I and Thou* concept of relationship. They were also impressed by the phenomenologic perspective that directed them to study the thing itself. The purpose behind their theory of nursing was to enrich the discipline by exploring and expanding the context of human experience and relationships.

Paterson and Zderad (1988) claim that nursing is an authentic commitment to nurturing human potential. It is an active choice by the nurse to be totally involved in the development and healing of another human being or group of human beings. Moreover, these nurse theorists claim that nurses are with other human beings at the most vulnerable and intimate times of their lives. Through a lived dialogue, each nurse becomes a *noetic locus* or knowing place, a place where awareness about self and other is fostered.

Holism   The view of holism put forth by Smuts in 1926 was, in his words, "neither of Science nor of Philosophy, but of some points of contact between the two" (p. v). Smuts suggested that the principle of holism is a factor that synthesizes and traces the wholes of things within the universe. "Evolution is nothing but the gradual development and stratification of progressive series of wholes, stretching from the inorganic beginnings to the highest levels of spiritual creation" (p. v). He stated that evolution was a progression of wholes spanning the primitive beginnings of inorganic substances through the highest realms of spiritual creations. In his first chapter, Smuts notes that the greatest gap in knowledge at the time of his writing is in the separations between matter, life, and mind. He adds that human life expresses a commingling of these phenomena, but the mechanistic viewpoint of science has forced them into discrete separations. He uses the terms *mind* and *soul* interchangeably. He points to the limitations of cause and effect reasoning to say "There could be nothing more in the effect than there was already in the cause; and if matter caused the soul, there could be nothing more in the soul than there already was in matter" (p. 9).

A basic assumption of holism is that situations, things, and events cannot maintain their integrity by reducing them to component parts when they are analyzed. Bits and pieces of the whole may be known and understood but they are different from the integrated whole. The holistic health movement emphasizes healing and maintenance of health where disease or illness is viewed as part of the whole; it is seen as a positive opportunity for growth.

In their book, *Holistic Nursing: A Handbook for Practice,* Dossey, Keegan, Guzzetta, and Kolkmeier (1988) emphasize that holism and healing are the essence of contemporary nursing. They express the belief that whole persons seek to reach their human potentials through inward journeys of self-discovery and self-understanding. They offer the circle as an ancient symbol of wholeness and present a model of human potential containing six equal wedges within the circle. Each wedge is an important component of the whole potential of human beings: relationships, spirit, mental, emotions, physical, and choices. They add that when the person is aware of the dynamic interplay among these parts, healing occurs.

The concept of holism in nursing literature has increased dramatically in the past 20 years. The term entered the nursing literature through the biopsychosocial approach of a psychiatrist, George Engel. Myra Levine is credited as the first nursing theorist to address this concept in her article published in 1971 in *Nursing Clinics of North America* in which she states that dualism and reductionism are not congruent with nursing's perspective of the whole person. Holism was often used interchangeably with the term *biopsychosocial* or as alternative approaches to Western medical health care. These two ideologies were merged in nursing literature as nurses sought advanced degrees and sought to develop a scientific and theoretical base for the professional discipline.

> Holism, with all its many facets, incorporates the empirical wisdom of the rural folk healer with the selflessness of the untrained nurse who knew the community, its residents, its economy, and its religious beliefs. Perhaps the message of holism in all its roles and disguises is that intuition, subjectivity, the value of the individual, caring, warmth, and compassion should be retained to some extent in research-based nursing that will inevitably become more specialized and reductionistic. (Sarkis & Skoner, 1987, p. 68)

Hover-Kramer (1989) explores the relevance of a transpersonal paradigm for nursing that recognizes the essential beginning of self-healing. She states that the search for wholeness in nursing is guarded by paradoxes; to be whole we must develop a reality greater than ourselves and surrender to this reality. This creates a tension between the present and timelessness and between the personal and the transpersonal. She notes that "creating a context for self-awareness and self-healing is most essential" (p. 30). She states we should begin by being kind to ourselves and give up self-criticism. "The path to healing requires us to move beyond our fragmented perceptions and to honor every part of our learning, to feel genuine compassion toward ourselves, and to release unrealistic self-expectations" (p. 33).

Holism serves as a philosophical framework for research on the phenomenon of comfort. Kolcaba, a nurse researcher, asserts that comfort is a complex and multidimensional personal experience that is difficult to measure but that is central to the discipline of nursing because it is related to the outcomes of nursing interventions (1991). Kolcaba's research has led to a more complete understanding of comfort as a holistic concept with physical, social, psychospiritual, and environmental dimensions. She states that comfort consists of having one's basic needs for ease, relief, and transcendence met. Kolcaba (1992) is currently developing instruments to measure this concept as a holistic phenomenon. She notes that holistic measurements have the following advantages over reductionist instruments:

1. They address interactions between physical and mental experiences

2. They account for differences in response to holistic interventions

3. They are appropriate for testing the effectiveness of holistic interventions

4. A single holistic instrument can replace the use of several more narrow measures

A great deal of nursing literature concerns the practice of holistic nursing. Although philosophic assumptions are rarely stated explicitly, common threads of beliefs and values about the multidimensional nature of the human being are readily apparent.

The concept of self-awareness for both nurse and client is evident in Susan Mayer's work entitled *Wholly Life: A New Perspective on Death* (1989). In this article, Mayer explores nurses' fears of death based on being powerless and/or annihilated. She then contrasts these with a new paradigm based on beliefs underlying the development of quantum physics. A principle of unity or oneness assumes that all of the universe constitutes an indivisible whole. Rather than persons being isolated and capable of extinction, the whole of the universe is contained in each of its parts. Holographic photography in which the whole picture is reflected by light shone on a single part is a concrete example of this principle. Mayer goes on to add that nurses can and do understand this unity of life through their experiences in self-exploration and in assisting others to expand their self-awareness. She asserts that for the nurse to assist a client who is afraid of dying, the nurse must first be aware of personal fears and communicate openly with the client. Consequences are that both client and nurse grow from this experience. This is another way of saying that healing takes place in the interrelationship between nurse and client.

Historicism   Historicism values human beings and their activities in the context of social culture and the passage of time. It has only recently played a valued part in the development of nursing knowledge and scholarship. With its roots in 19th-century Germany, historicism provides a perspective of human existence influenced by social and political systems at a particular time and place. This view supports the study of past human events that were recorded and that can be interpreted to shed light on current and future events. The assumption is not to discover laws about human existence but rather to describe the structure of human phenomena by piecing together evidence from the past. Historicism asserts that desirable values and practices within a human society may be advanced through exploration of past events. Its influence can be seen not only in the development of nursing science but in further understanding and promoting of the art of nursing. Historiography is a method for developing nursing knowledge that is based on this philosophy and that can be of great benefit to the discipline (Sarnecky, 1990).

The ideas of Laudan (1977) have strongly influenced the development of nursing history as an important component of the discipline. Laudan espouses an evolutionary approach to knowledge development and asserts that understanding process is of greater value than product (Sarnecky, 1990). Qualitative methods are then used to enlarge a discipline's understanding about current issues. Nurse researchers have successfully used these methods to enhance our understanding of traditional nursing attitudes and practices such as those of nurses in World War I, domestic tasks associated with a nursing role, and images of nurses in movies (Beeber, 1990; Hughes, 1990; Stevens, 1990).

Feminism   Feminist theories developed in response to philosophies such as humanism, which valued the male intellect and education for males. Liberal feminists of the 1800s believed in the equality of males and females and in the ability of education to advance society. Bunting and Campbell, nurse researchers at Wayne State University in Detroit, trace the history of nursing and feminism. They note that equality and autonomy have been rare for nurses in the patriarchal systems of religious and military establishments where they functioned historically (Bunting & Campbell, 1990). Nursing, however, is one of the oldest professions and is characterized by feminine qualities of nurturing and caring usually associated with mothers. Midwifery, for example, was historically controlled by women until medicine became more formalized and dominated the health care delivery system in the United States. Similarly, in the United States, early training of nurses was under the direction of medicine rather than that of autonomous nurse educators such as Nightingale established in England. More recently, cultural feminism espoused the beliefs that males and females are different not only in terms of physiology but also in terms of thinking and making decisions, whereas radical feminism is based on beliefs about the oppression of women (Doering, 1992). This variety of philosophical feminist assumptions may have a profound influence on the place of awareness in the healing practices of males and females.

Peggy Chinn writes of a dream in which she entered a place called a Healing House (1989). She had gone there because her body was not functioning properly, but she was uncertain about what to expect. While there, she met nurses who were kind and taught her how to relax and bring calm, peaceful messages to her body. This dream introduces Chinn's description of nursing's patterns of knowing that contribute to, and are contributed to by, feminist thinking. She states that changes that are needed in the health care system will not come from the power base that nursing has (or more realistically, perhaps, does not have), but can come from philosophies of nursing that reflect the ideal dream with which she begins this description. Chinn refers to health as wholeness and adds that this is an idea worthy of nursing's highest attention and effort. She adds that nursing can achieve alteration in health care delivery because it acknowledges various patterns of knowing. More will be said about this in chapter 5. Chinn's dream demonstrates application of historicism in reflecting on past and present conditions with a vision toward needed change in the future.

Idealism The doctrine that thoughts or ideas constitute the fundamental reality of life is known as idealism. In contrast to materialism, which holds that matter is the primary truth or reality, idealism denies the primacy of matter. Idealism is found in metaphysics and ethics. Sarter (1987) argues that idealism is an appropriate metaphysical foundation for a holistic nursing science because it assumes consciousness is of central importance in understanding human beings within the universe. She adds that this philosophy encompasses the range of human experiences and does not separate fact from value in those experiences. She points to the importance of this philosophy as supporting nursing conceptual models such as those of Rogers, Paterson and Zderad, Watson, Parse, Newman, and Travelbee. With respect to Rogers's conceptualization of the life process, evolutionary idealism, according to Sarter, "interprets the purpose of evolution to be the unfolding of consciousness" (p. 5), which is also consistent with Newman's definition of health as *expanding consciousness.* Sarter also claims that a "specific, testable nursing theory that could be derived from a philosophy of evolutionary idealism is that experiences of health and illness can promote the development of greater knowledge, feeling, or volition in the individual" (p. 6). The purpose of nursing, then, would be to facilitate this evolutionary development of consciousness in the client (Sarter, 1987).

Nursing theorist Margaret Newman of the University of Minnesota views health as expanding consciousness (1986). In this view, disease is merely a pattern or manifestation of the whole and part of the expanding of consciousness. There is a rhythmic cycle or evolution of order and disorder that goes in the direction of greater complexity. Nursing, according to Newman, must help persons to identify the patterns of their interaction with the environment and to "bring about attunement to higher consciousness, is the process of sensing into one's own being" (1989, p. 4), which she says is consistent with a holographic view where each part contains information about the whole. She advocates the process of focusing awareness so that there is congruence between emotional and physical feeling. Nursing helps people become aware of these patterns through interaction. In such a healing interaction, the nurse is fully present and offers the whole self for an authentic relationship in which the two, in Newman's words, "resonate with the consciousness of the universe" (1989, p. 6).

Philosophies for Nursing Science and Practice

Each of the philosophies presented here may be found in the comprehensive nursing literature of the past 50 years. Each has been useful in the development of nursing theories, knowledge, and practice. Table 2.1 depicts one way in which nursing's

Dimension of Human Being	Philosophical Approaches
Physical	Empiricism
	Reductionism
	Logical positivism
	Holism
Psychological/developmental	Existentialism
	Humanism
	Phenomenology
	Holism
	Idealism
Social/interactional	Feminism
	Historicism
	Holism
	Idealism
	Phenomenology
Spiritual	Phenomenology
	Holism
	Idealism

TABLE 2.1   *Philosophies Related to Multiple Dimensions of Human Beings*

unique worldview is related to the multidimensionality of human beings and the various philosophies that have been useful to nursing.

Nursing's unique worldview is a synthesis of ideas, beliefs, and values provided by the many different philosophical perspectives outlined in table 2.1. The physical dimension of human beings is a focal point for nursing care. The tenets of empiricism and reductionism have contributed to organizing knowledge about the structure and function of the human body, which is essential to the practice of nursing. The addition of holism reflects nursing's view that the physical body cannot be isolated from the social and cultural context into which one is born and in which one lives, thinks, learns, and develops. Holism embraces whole persons and their mutual relationships with the universe. This worldview sees the integration of body and mind-spirit with the universe as the ultimate truth. Similarly, existentialism is relevant to nursing practice because it emphasizes the value of human love and care and the meaningfulness of relationships. Phenomenology and idealism emphasize further the ideas that life processes are integrated and have meaning.

The philosophies of feminism and historicism are relevant to the experiences of human beings over time. Each person is born at a specified moment in time and location in space. All the events between the person's birth and death are thus relevant to other happenings grounded in chronology. The physical body reflects chronological changes as biorhythms or circadian fluctuations of body chemicals and functions. The social context or culture into which each human being is born, lives, and dies reflects the importance of human relationships. Feminism is but one philosophy that emphasizes the significance of interpersonal relationships on the individual's potential for healing. Similarly, existentialism and humanism support authentic interpersonal relationships between human beings as the basis for a healing and healthy universe.

The intellectual-spiritual dimension of human beings is reflected in the assumptions and beliefs expressed through a philosophy of idealism. Consciousness is identified as the primary reality of the universe; as an individual's consciousness unfolds, healing is made possible.

Summary of Nursing Philosophy

The philosophies presented briefly here do not include all philosophical thoughts and doctrines that influence nursing science and practice. However, they represent many of the ideas that have influenced the development of nursing theory and clinical nursing practice. Table 2.2 provides summaries of the major tenets of each worldview and the aims of the philosophies.

On the brink of a new century, nursing can reflect upon the use of multiple philosophies for the purposes of identifying the focus of expertise in nursing and for developing as a profession. Such pluralism has helped to clarify boundaries and assert the worth of healing processes. What remains to be done is to continue to pose philosophical questions within the discipline. Beginning with awareness of those worldviews that have influenced thinking and acting within the nursing profession, the discipline can move into a new century of vision about the importance of healing to individuals and the universe as a whole.

Philosophy	Major Tenets	Aims
Empiricism	Truth comes from observation and experience.	Describe, predict, and control.
	Science is value-free.	Determine cause-effect.
	Theory is either true or false.	
Existentialism	Humans have value because they exist.	Describe human condition.
	Love and care are universal forces.	
	Meaning is in authentic interpersonal relationships.	
Feminism	Women are as valued as men.	Confront systematic injustices.
	There are basic differences between men and women.	Respect differences.
Phenomenology	All life processes are integrated and have meaning.	Understand the essential meaning of experiences.
	There are multiple modes of awareness.	
Holism	Evolution is a progression of wholes.	Understand human: irreducible whole constantly changing and evolving.
	Things and events are understood only as irreducible wholes.	
Historicism	Human values and practices advance through examination of the past.	Describe human existence in context of social culture and passage of time.
Idealism	Ideas or thoughts constitute reality.	Human beings' consciousness resonates with the universe.
	Consciousness expands toward greater order and complexity.	

TABLE 2.2   *Summary of Philosophies Contributing to Nursing Science and Practice, Tenets, and Aims*

PHILOSOPHY, SCIENCE, AND THE PRACTICE OF HEALING

Philosophy is distinguished from science and practice. Philosophy addresses underlying questions that are not answered through the systematic methods of science. Rather, philosophical issues deal with assumptions that cannot be proven or disproved. These assumptions direct the development of science, which, in turn, guides healing practices. Moreover, philosophy considers meaning and interpretation as centrally important, whereas science considers the rigors of coherence and logical ordering of ideas as centrally important. Philosophy consists of those statements about beliefs, values, and attitudes that are consistent with the development of a specific science. The science of healing, which may not be the primary claim of any single discipline, rests on beliefs and values about the nature of human beings and their relationships with the entire universe. Ideas about healing processes form a science as these ideas are translated into concepts that can be observed and/or measured in some way, shown to be related to one another, and then used to influence healing practices by those who wish to use the science.

Nursing theorists suggest that a metaparadigm includes a set of concepts significant to the discipline, identifies a point of view taken by members of the discipline, and outlines appropriate methodologies for conducting research on the phenomena of concern. A metaparadigm is a "fundamental worldview agreed upon by all members of the discipline" (Sarter, 1987, p. 3). Nursing has not yet identified a unified perspective that is unique to the discipline. However, there is general agreement that nursing is a process and includes the idea of healing.

Beliefs about healing belong to nurses and their clients alike. These beliefs may be similar or different and reflect the three types of awareness presented in chapter 1. Awareness of one's own philosophy about human life and its relationship to the universe as a whole affects the decisions and actions taken by either nurse or client to facilitate or hinder healing. A personal philosophy consists of what one believes about reality, causation, good and harm, freedom, rights, and responsibilities. It includes what one values and what one expects from self and others.

Much of an individual's philosophy or worldview lies outside of cognitive awareness but is a strong influence on attitudes and behaviors expressed by the individual in myriad ways.

Similarly, a professional philosophy or worldview consists of what the collected body of the profession believes to be true. Such a worldview influences the development of the science and/or art unique to that discipline and includes the beliefs and values shared by members of that discipline. Mature professional disciplines such as mathematics and chemistry reflect a unified worldview, whereas less well-developed professions such as nursing reflect a more diversified worldview wherein philosophical assumptions from various schools of thought are used for the discipline.

What did Nightingale mean when she said *only nature cures*? What is nature anyway? This is a first-order philosophical question and far beyond the scope of this book. However, this brief review of philosophies for and of nursing offers some insight into a possible answer to this question. Nature is not just a thing that can be observed or measured through the senses. We may be able to learn much about nature with empirical methods of observation. However, nature is complex and dynamic; it is the whole of life and the many processes that connect lives through time and space. If Nightingale is correct and only nature cures, then it is through harmonizing with the whole of living processes that one is healed and experiences health.

Watson's theory includes the statement that nursing's role is to help the person "gain more self-knowledge, self-control, and readiness for self-healing" (1988, p. 35). This suggests that the nurse promotes self-awareness in the nursing client. Watson refers to health as "unity and harmony within the mind, body, and soul" (p. 48). She adds that health is associated with "the degree of congruence between the self as perceived and the self as experienced" (p. 48). She identifies the goal of nursing to help persons gain a higher degree of harmony that generates "self-knowledge, self-reverence, self-healing, and self-care processes while allowing increasing diversity" (p. 49). This goal is met through caring processes and transactions. As Watson notes in these assumptions, nursing has historically been aware of the needs of human beings for love and care. She adds that the profession itself must be aware of its own needs with respect to these two concepts and treat the members of the discipline in this way. Her focus is on the interpersonal aspects of caring as the perspective most central to and agreed upon by members of the nursing discipline.

Philosophically, Orem, a nursing theorist, seeks to integrate the human mind, body, and soul; reality and fantasy; facts and meaning; objective and subjective worlds; external and internal events; disease and health; and physical and metaphysical realms. She also identifies mutuality as a moral foundation of nursing (Orem, 1985). This stresses the importance of relationship between nurse and client as healing takes place. Orem adds that "awareness and knowledge about one's need for care" are necessary for caring to occur (p. 32).

Watson's theory of caring and Orem's theory of self-care point to the value of developing awareness for healing. Each of these nurse theorists emphasizes the multidimensional nature of human beings. This supports the thesis of this book that healing is related to developing cognitive, intuitive, and transcendent awareness. Cognitive awareness of physical structure and function flows out of the basic sciences built on philosophies of empiricism and positivism and the importance of social context that comes from a philosophy of historicism. Intuitive awareness of the wholeness of life flows from existentialism, holism, and phenomenology. Transcendent awareness is based primarily on ideas presented in phenomenology and idealism. Each type of awareness may be developed for healing.

The example of Joshua and Cheryl presented at the beginning of this chapter reflects nursing's synthesis and application of knowledge based on many of the tenets of these philosophies. Much of what nurses know about the physiology of asthma in children and the human response to specific medications and respiratory treatments comes from scientific inquiry based on principles of empiricism and positivism. The empirical worldview allows scientists to predict and control physical events associated with physiological processes such as narrowing of airways and production of excessive mucus in response to environmental irritants. Existentialism and phenomenology emphasize that human beings have universal needs for love and care. Meaningful living experiences come from authentic interpersonal relationships in which neither participant is reduced from an *I* to an *it*. These philosophical stances enable Cheryl, the nurse, to understand the lived experience of a child who has asthma as part of a larger, integrated universe. The child is not reduced to so many mechanical parts that need to be fixed when they break down. Similarly, holism allows Cheryl to consider the many dimensions of Joshua and the other children in her care at the campsite. Historicism permits her to view her own life and those of the children from a perspective of the past, present, and future and the unique context in which they are now living and interacting. Each child brings past experiences that influence present attitudes and behaviors and each comes with expectations about the future. Considering the tenets of idealism, Cheryl can view healing as a natural process of harmonizing the children and herself with the universe at large.

As nursing continues to evolve and develop as a discipline, philosophies of art and science are used as the basis for conceptual models and theories of nursing. For example, positivism contributes certain principles to what we know about physical healing of the body. Existentialism contributes to our understanding of interpersonal relationships (e.g., social support) and the part that this authenticity plays in relationships that contribute to healing. It also influences the development of our ethics and our ability to do what is good. Another example of existentialism as the basis for nursing theory is the theory of mastery described by Janet Younger (1991). Younger asserts that the way humans respond to stressful or difficult situations is an existential problem. One type of response is mastery in which the individual gains competency, control, and dominion over the stressful experience. This mastery is expressed both intrapersonally (within oneself) and interpersonally (between persons). Mastery also contributes to growth of the individual and, therefore, can also be conceptualized as a human healing phenomenon.

Phenomenology contributes to our understanding of the essence or meaning of the lived experiences of human beings. As Rose's study of the inner strength of women shows, this philosophy influences our understanding and interpretation of the healing process (1990). The women in Rose's study demonstrated cognitive awareness in accepting their physical and sociocultural limitations through a process of introspection. They demonstrated intuitive awareness in understanding the complexity of their lives and finding meaning in difficult situations. Moreover, they demonstrated transcendent awareness through centering and being quiet, thus feeling their connections and harmonization with the universe.

Johnson asserts that the way nursing is viewed as a science is relevant to the art of nursing (1991). She argues that nursing should be conceptualized as a practical science rather than as a basic or applied science. Knowledge in a practical science is developed to achieve particular objectives. Johnson provides definitions for each of these types of sciences and defines practical science as one that is applicable to performing specified tasks. She provides assumptions about the epistemology of nursing science. Johnson further asserts that "nursing science must ultimately serve the art of nursing and not the reverse" (Johnson, 1991, p. 9). She notes that in nursing practice, nurses apply scientific knowledge in addition to their personal insights about the situation or tasks at hand. This reflects both the science and the art of nursing.

References

Allan, J. D. (1988). Knowing what to weigh: Women's self-care activities related to weight. *Advances in Nursing Science, 11* (1), 47–60.

Beeber, L. S. (1990). To be one of the boys: Aftershocks of the World War I nursing experiences. *Advances in Nursing Science, 12* (4), 32–43.

Buber, M. (1970). *I and thou.* New York: Charles Scribner's Sons.

Bunting, S., & Campbell, J. C. (1990). Feminism and nursing: Historical perspectives. *Advances in Nursing Science, 12* (4), 11–24.

Chinn, P. L. (1989). Nursing patterns of knowing and feminist thought. *Nursing & Health Care, 10* (2), 71–75.

Clinton, J. F., Denyes, M. J., Goodwin, J. O., & Koto, E. M. (1977). Developing criterion measures of nursing care: Case study of a process. *Journal of Nursing Administration, 7* (7), 41–45.

Doering, L. (1992). Power and knowledge in nursing: A feminist post-structuralist view. *Advances in Nursing Science, 14* (4), 24–33.

Dossey, B. M., Keegan, L., Guzzetta, C. E., & Kolkmeier, L. G. (1988). *Holistic nursing: A handbook for practice.* Rockville, MD: Aspen Publishers, Inc.

Feigl, H. (1973). Positivism in the twentieth century (logical empiricism). In P. P. Wiener (Ed.), *Dictionary of the history of ideas, Vol. III* (pp. 545–551). New York: Charles Scribner's Sons, Publishers.

Heidegger, M. (1972). *On time and being.* New York: Harper & Row Publishers.

Henderson, V. (1966). *The nature of nursing.* New York: Macmillan.

Hover-Kramer, D. (1989). Creating a context for self-healing: The transpersonal perspective. *Holistic Nursing Practice, 3* (3), 27–34.

Hughes, L. (1990). Professionalizing domesticity: A synthesis of selected nursing historiography. *Advances in Nursing Science, 12* (4), 25–31.

Husserl, E. (1962). *Ideas: General introduction to pure phenomenology.* New York: Collier Books.

Johnson, J. L. (1991). Nursing science: Basic, applied, or practical? Implications for the art of nursing. *Advances in Nursing Science, 14* (1), 7–16.

Kauffman, S. A. (1993). *The origins of order.* New York: Oxford University Press.

Kolcaba, K. Y. (1991). A taxonomic structure for the concept comfort. *Image: Journal of Nursing Scholarship, 23,* 237–240.

Kolcaba, K. Y. (1992). Holistic comfort: Operationalizing the construct as a nurse-sensitive outcome. *Advances in Nursing Science, 15* (1), 1–10.

Laudan, L. (1977). *Progress and its problems: Towards a theory of scientific growth.* Berkcley, CA: University of California Press.

Levine, M. (1971). Holistic nursing. *Nursing Clinics of North America, 6* (2), 253–264.

Mayer, S. (1989). Wholly life: A new perspective on death. *Holistic Nursing Practice, 3* (4), 72–80.

Newman, M. A. (1986). *Health as expanding consciousness.* St. Louis: The C. V. Mosby Company.

Newman, M. A. (1989). The spirit of nursing. *Holistic Nursing Practice, 3* (3), 1–6.

Nightingale, F. (1946). *Notes on nursing: What it is, and what it is not.* Philadelphia: J. B. Lippincott Company.

Orem, D. E. (1985). *Nursing: Concepts of practice* (3rd ed.). New York: McGraw-Hill Book Company.

Paterson, J. G., & Zderad, L. T. (1988). *Humanistic nursing.* New York: National League for Nursing.

Rew, L. (1990). Childhood sexual abuse: Toward a self-care framework for nursing intervention and research. *Archives of Psychiatric Nursing, 4* (3), 147–153.

Roach, M. S. (1987). *The human act of caring: A blueprint for the health professions.* Ottawa: Canadian Hospital Association.

Rogers, M. E. (1970). *An introduction to the theoretical basis of nursing*. Philadelphia: F. A. Davis Company.

Rose, J. F. (1990). Psychologic health of women: A phenomenologic study of women's inner strength. *Advances in Nursing Science, 12* (2), 56–70.

Sarkis, J. M., & Skoner, M. M. (1987). An analysis of the concept of holism in nursing literature. *Holistic Nursing Practice, 2* (1), 61–69.

Sarnecky, M. T. (1990). Historiography: A legitimate research methodology for nursing. *Advances in Nursing Science, 12* (4), 1–10.

Sarter, B. (1987). Evolutionary idealism: A philosophical foundation for holistic nursing theory. *Advances in Nursing Science, 9* (2), 1–9.

Sarter, B. (1988). *The stream of becoming: A study of Martha Rogers's theory*. New York: The National League for Nursing.

Smuts, J. C. (1926). *Holism and evolution*. New York: The Macmillan Company.

Stevens, S. Y. (1990). Sale of the century: Images of nursing in the Movietonews during World War II. *Advances in Nursing Science, 12* (4), 44–52.

Watson, J. (1988). *Nursing: Human science and human care. A theory of nursing*. New York: The National League for Nursing.

Younger, J. B. (1991). A theory of mastery. *Advances in Nursing Science, 14* (1), 76–89.

Suggested Reading

Cramer, S. (1992). The nature of history: Meditations on Clio's craft. *Nursing Research, 41* (1), 4–7.

Hempel, C. G. (1966). *Philosophy of natural science*. Englewood Cliffs, NJ: Prentice-Hall, Inc.

Jacox, A. K., & Webster, G. (1986). Competing theories of science. In L. H. Nicoll (Ed.), *Perspectives on nursing theory* (pp. 335–341). Boston: Little, Brown and Company.

Meleis, A. I. (1991). *Theoretical nursing: Development and progress*. Philadelphia: J. B. Lippincott Company.

Moccia, P. (1988). A critique of compromise: Beyond the methods debate. *Advances in Nursing Science, 10* (4), 1–9.

Nagle, L. M., & Mitchell, G. J. (1991). Theoretic diversity: Evolving paradigmatic issues in research and practice. *Advances in Nursing Science, 14* (1), 17–25.

Newman, M. (1989). The spirit of nursing. *Holistic Nursing Practice, 3* (3), 1–6.

Reverby, S. (1987). A caring dilemma: Womanhood and nursing in historical perspective. *Nursing Research, 36* (1), 5–11.

Salsberry, P. J. (1991). A philosophy of nursing: What is it? What is it not? In J. F. Kikuchi & H. Simmons (Eds.), *Developing a philosophy of nursing* (pp. 11–19). Thousand Oaks, CA: Sage Publications.

Schumacher, K. L., & Gortner, S.R. (1992). (Mis)conceptions and reconceptions about traditional science. *Advances in Nursing Science, 14* (4), 1–11.

Silva, M. C. (1977). Philosophy, science, theory: Interrelationships and implications for nursing research. *IMAGE: Journal of Nursing Scholarship, 9* (3), 59–63.

Whall, A. L. (1989). The influence of logical positivism on nursing practice. *Image: Journal of Nursing Scholarship, 21*, 243–245.

Woodhouse, M. B. (1990). *A preface to philosophy* (4th ed.). Belmont, CA: Wadsworth Publishing Company.

Zahourek, R. P. (1987). Clinical hypnosis in holistic nursing. *Holistic Nursing Practice, 2* (1), 15–24.

BARRIERS TO
AWARENESS AND
HEALING

*To accommodate the requirements of scientism, we
break into parts things that should be viewed as
wholes and we separate items that might better be
understood as complementary.*

Philip Goldberg, 1983

Harriet and Ann

Harriet was 74 years old when she was hospitalized for a vague syndrome of stomach distress. Harriet was a widow for 7 years before
meeting Jonathan. Jonathan and Harriet met through mutual friends
and she was swept off her feet by the variety of activities they
enjoyed together. After a short 3-week courtship, Jonathan and
Harriet married, but the whirlwind romance came to a screeching
halt. Soon after the honeymoon, Harriet began to experience nausea
and occasional diarrhea. Within 2 months, these symptoms increased
both in frequency and severity. She lost her appetite and began to
feel despondent. Jonathan settled into a routine of quiet passivity.

Harriet finally made an appointment with her physician who began by treating the obvious symptoms. However, she soon decided to hospitalize Harriet for observation and tests. The physician, a long-time friend of Harriet, suspected that the vague syndrome of stomach distress might possibly be masking the real cause of Harriet's discomfort. She requested that a nurse counselor visit Harriet and provide consultation. In the meantime, all the ordered tests of bodily fluids and functions returned with normal results.

When the staff nurse, Ann, first met Harriet, the small woman was sitting in bed wearing only a hospital gown and her glasses. To the nurse, she looked frightened and fragile. Her shoulders were rounded and her head hung sadly down to one side. As they talked, Harriet rubbed her stomach, covered her mouth with her hand, and shook her head slowly from side to side as the nurse asked her to tell her about her recent marriage and honeymoon. Harriet sobbed quietly as she gradually looked into the nurse's eyes and said, "I'm sorry, but quite frankly, Jonathan just turns my stomach!" She added, "I know he doesn't really love me, but I wanted to find love so badly, I guess I just put on blinders. Now I get nauseous every time I think of my mistake and how this will hurt my family."

Within 48 hours of her admission to the hospital, and with the encouragement of Ann and her physician, Harriet focused her awareness on what she was really feeling and on her beliefs about the expectations of her family. She realized that the symptoms of stomach distress were a literal translation of her true feelings about Jonathan and that they served to distract her and those around her from the painful reality of her premature decision to marry Jonathan. Harriet believed that she could gain the support from her family only if she were legitimately in need of their support — as in being ill and hospitalized. The symptoms and the hospitalization did give her time away from Jonathan and she was then able to engage in self-reflection. As her anxiety decreased, her perception of her plight increased. She became aware of her true feelings, her beliefs, and her behavioral response of hiding behind physical illness to deal with an important interpersonal problem. She left the hospital free from her symptoms of abdominal distress and with the resolve to address her husband and family directly about what she needed to re-establish harmony in her life.

Initially, Harriet lacked the cognitive awareness of how physical symptoms of disease could be a literal reflection of her feelings. She also lacked cognitive awareness of the kind of support her family would give her if she admitted that she had made a mistake in marrying Jonathan. With time alone for reflection and introspection, Harriet not only developed the cognitive awareness she originally lacked, but recognized an intuitive awareness that enabled her to understand the meaning of her symptoms within the larger context of her sociocultural background and life history. This type of awareness reassured her that healing was possible even if she didn't know precisely how that would happen. Moreover, as Harriet began to overcome the barriers that interfered with her cognitive and intuitive awareness, she began to realize again that her life had a spiritual dimension that went beyond the physical and sociocultural parameters that defined her current situation.

BARRIERS TO AWARENESS

A barrier is anything that interferes with movement toward a desired end. A barrier may be any type of obstacle along one's path or a boundary that prevents a person from gaining access to life's treasures. The concept of healing as it is discussed in this book is based on the assumption that human beings desire health and value healing as a process that contributes to this goal. Another assumption is that a person's awareness of self and connections with others promote the healing process and form the stepping stones in the journey toward wholeness and harmony with the environment. Barriers, thus, are the obstacles that prevent people from living lives of wholeness and harmony. Any situation that limits the development of personal awareness acts as a barrier in the healing process.

Many factors hinder the healing process by interfering with a person's awareness. These factors include cultural beliefs and values, emotions, social conditions and institutions, and specific patterns of behavioral responses to the everyday challenges of living. Beliefs are deeply ingrained through the various experiences in a person's life and form the basic worldview or personal philosophy that eventually colors all of a person's perceptions of life's happenings. Beliefs are reinforced by family, friends, and the culture at large, including the status of that culture within its geographic location. Although they may never be challenged through formal reasoning, beliefs form the values that guide a person's decisions to act or not act in specific ways. Beliefs that are threatened or disputed by other people are accompanied by strong emotions that may lead to peculiar activities to decrease the anxiety that accompanies such threats. Threats or challenges to a person's belief system emphasize the separation rather than the union between people, thus forming barriers to harmonious interpersonal relationships.

When people are fully aware of their beliefs and values, they have an understanding of how they interpret the world around them. This self-awareness also enables them to understand that their personal perceptions of the world may differ from those of other people. Consequently, they also understand how their minds and bodies, and the minds and bodies of others, respond to provocation and competition from the environment. The external environment poses a variety of threats and challenges to people, particularly when people encounter unknown areas or situations. Personal responses to a new or strange environment include changes within the body that usually lie outside a person's ordinary awareness. For example, when a person is accidentally scratched by a thorny bush when walking in the woods, the body's immune system begins to work in such a way as to fight off microorganisms that could destroy tissue. Inflammation in the form of redness and swelling in the part of the body that is scratched occurs without the person being consciously aware of the need for such a response. When the person sees the inflammatory response, however, she recognizes this process as the beginning of healing. This realization may be accompanied by other conscious responses of alarm or calm. If the person's outlook on life is basically negative and self-destructive, that person may interpret this response as a nuisance or evidence that life is difficult and that she must continuously be on guard. This type of outlook is based on an assumption of separation between oneself and the world rather than of unity of life. Beliefs about division and detachment will hinder the healing process in those with this type of outlook. In cultures where people value their relationships of harmony with the environment, positive responses reflect other beliefs that promote health and well-being. Emotions such as fear and anxiety interfere with awareness because they narrow perceptions and exhaust limited energy resources.

Social conditions such as poverty at one extreme and affluence at the other extreme emphasize disharmony rather than harmony among people. Such conditions illuminate the differences between people rather than the commonalities. Poverty prevents people from experiencing the fruits of humanity's intelligence and hard work. It exists as a class of barriers that prevent people from enjoying their full human potential of health and harmonious living. Similarly, affluence that is characterized by overstimulation from an environment that sends ambiguous and conflicting messages about what is valued and what is expected of persons forms another type of barrier to healing awareness. Both classes of social barriers can lead to an inability of persons to focus on healing harmony. Social institutions whose purpose is to contribute to the health and welfare of citizens often contribute more to illness and prevent healing by creating obstacles to those desiring access to them. Institutions such as governmental agencies, public schools, and hospitals with their proverbial red tape often erect hurdles to the very services they were created to provide. Such institutions often contribute to separation and competition rather than to community and harmony.

Cultural Values and Beliefs

In chapter 2, the basic philosophies of healing that influence a person's values and beliefs were presented. In this chapter, beliefs and values, those things that we pay attention to the most, are discussed in the context of the person's ethnic culture, community, and family. Before we are able to reason and think for ourselves, our traditional culture and family of origin begin to exert powerful influences on our basic systems of beliefs and values. The ways in which we view our bodies, express our emotions, respond to our environments, and spend our time are molded by those around us. This molding strengthens what the culture wants us to see and prevents us from seeing what the culture does not want us to see. For example, in a culture that reveres the elderly, infants and young children learn early on to respect the aging process and to see it as a positive aspect of living. In contrast, youngsters in a culture that values the vigor and beauty of youth learn to dread the physical and mental indicators of advancing age. Such beliefs, which may be addressed directly and openly or indirectly and subtly, have a powerful impact on the development of a child's awareness of self within the culture, the community, and the family. Thus, ethnic cultures broadly define what is of greater or lesser importance, and families are the microcosm in which such cultural mores and rituals are instilled. From infancy throughout the lifespan, the culture, community, and family determine, in large measure, the values and beliefs that a person embraces. These basic values and beliefs contribute much to a personal sense of identity and health.

Freud's psychoanalytic theory, including the phenomena of defense mechanisms, focuses on those situations and ideas that a person allows into awareness. The concept of repression is based on the assumption that a person rejects from consciousness those thoughts or memories that are too painful to remember. Repression, thus, limits how a person experiences the world as a whole by controlling what the person allows into awareness (Faber, 1981). Experiences from childhood influence the way in which people perceive the world and their places in it. These experiences begin with sensory input and physical sensations as the infant receives and responds to the environment of other people and things within it. The complex interrelationships between mind and body form the beginnings of our perceptions and awareness of the world as a safe or unsafe place in which to live. Those situations that foster safety and connectedness between people and events contribute to healthy development. In contrast, those situations that emphasize separation are painful and constrict the development of supportive, growth-inducing networks.

Strong cultural beliefs and values influence the development of perceptual awareness in the members of each social and ethnic culture. Similarly, these traditional values and beliefs influence the development of social institutions that further reinforce those to which the members of that society attend. America has traditionally been characterized as a melting pot of peoples who have come here seeking new freedoms and opportunities and an escape from oppressive belief systems and traditions. Consequently, a variety of new ways of viewing the world and the human being's place in it have evolved in America through the process of blending and sifting a variety of old ways of seeing and doing things.

Recently, however, newer groups of immigrants have spoken out in favor of retaining their original ethnic identities, beliefs, and values, at times creating conflict and tensions with other ethnic groups. When different belief and value systems within a society are perceived as conflictual, tension and confusion arise among the cultural groups of that society. This tension and confusion is stressful to people, and it narrows their perceptual awareness, often leading to disharmony and illness. Whereas the view of American society as a melting pot emphasized the blending of many ideas and hopes into a new way of life, the coexistence of multiple cultural groups, whose ideas and hopes are very different from one another, does not lead smoothly to a clear way of being in the world. Each ethnic group, wanting to hold onto its traditional and cherished beliefs, does not necessarily share enough beliefs with the dominant cultural group to form a new society of harmony. What exists here is a barrier to mutual understanding and respect due to the perception or misperception of dissimilar views and values. What is lacking here is a mutual desire to engage in a creative dialectic that forges a new and better way of living together. Such a situation is a barrier to healing within individuals and groups.

The vignette about Harriet at the beginning of this chapter illustrates the effect of an ethnic culture on the lived experience of a person. Harriet believed that her family would not be willing or able to give her the emotional support she needed to admit her mistake of marrying Jonathan. Without consciously acknowledging this belief and the fear that accompanied it, her body automatically took over and created a response that was acceptable within her culture in general and her family in particular. Family and friends would rally to comfort and assist her at a time of illness. But she feared that they would not stand by her if she admitted that she had made a mistake about marriage. In her culture and family, marriage was a sacred institution and she had made vows in public about her commitment to stay in this relationship until she or Jonathan died. To revoke this vow was unthinkable. Yet, to stay in a marriage that was not motivated by a true feeling of love and devotion was to be untrue to herself, and Harriet's body would not let her get away with this self-deception!

Human Emotions

The vignette about Harriet also illustrates the power of emotions to produce barriers to both awareness and healing. Fear and anxiety are natural and protective emotions. They are associated with strong physiological changes within the body that are difficult to ignore. In general, the autonomic nervous system springs into action when we perceive a danger from the environment. The natural instinct to fight or to run away from harm, real or imagined, is built into the very fabric of our human responses. However, when the emotions of fear or anxiety are ignored, the physiological accompaniments remain even when we trick our minds into believing there is no danger or no need for cautious response. When consciousness of situations is too painful, the mind represses the truth and erects a barricade to awareness that, in spite of being painful, could lead to healing.

The pioneering work of Selye (1956/1976) provides evidence of the strong link between perceptual awareness, thinking, and physiological responses. In his conceptualization of the general adaptation syndrome, Selye outlines the stress response as consisting of three parts:

1. Activation of the sympathetic portion of the autonomic nervous system
2. Activation of the endocrine system and the release of powerful pituitary and adrenal chemicals
3. Suppression of the immune system

Although the environment produces many stressors that act upon all people such as natural catastrophes, including earthquakes, tornadoes, and floods, people perceive and think about these situations differently. They experience the stress response in different ways because of the meaning of these events to them.

Rossi and Cheek (1988) propose that stress is experienced within the body as communication of information involving the brain, autonomic nervous system, endocrine system, and immune system. This communication is transmitted by chemicals known as neurotransmitters, which are released in various parts of the body. Such communication takes place at an unconscious level. Rossi and Cheek believe that healing can occur through consciously facilitating these unconscious communication processes among body systems. Again, self-understanding of how one's body responds to changes within the environment is an essential ingredient in healing. Anything that interferes with this self-understanding acts as a barrier to the healing process.

The physiological responses to fear include the release of powerful chemicals into the blood stream. These chemicals alter the usual pattern of blood flow and oxygen consumption. Every bit of physical energy focuses on survival of the host. When the fear-inducing stimulus is removed, the body's defense system usually returns to a resting state. However, if left unchecked, these chemical resources begin to take their toll on the very body they were produced to protect. Chemicals that were designed to be used for an occasional emergency accumulate with toxic effects when the fear-producing stimulus remains in a person's perception. The human body cannot long sustain exposure to such potent substances and begins to respond by developing internal symptoms of malfunction or disease. A person's awareness of her view of the world, perception and interpretation of events, and internal physiological responses can support the healing process or interrupt this natural tendency.

The physiological responses to fear can be maintained in the presence of an imagined threat or fear as well as in the presence of a real dangerous beast. The human mind learns to differentiate between danger that really exists in the environment and that which exists only in imagination. When a fearful stimulus from the environment is no longer present, as in the case of a tiger jumping into a person's path from behind a tree, physiological responses naturally return to normal. However, when a person continues to hold the fearful stimulus in imagination, a pervasive type of anxiety is experienced and the human mind begins to experience confusion about whether a real or imaginary tiger exists. When the person believes that the danger is real, but the tiger really does not lurk along the path, the person's perceptual awareness will narrow and set up a process where the chemical response within the body is identical to the situation involving the real tiger.

Other emotions in addition to fear are accompanied by the release of chemical agents that have the potential to save or destroy the human body. Anger is associated with gathering one's strength to attack a perceived or actual threat from another. Like fear, anger is usually time-limited and quickly dissipates with the direct expression of the emotion. Yet, many people fail to fully acknowledge angry feelings, are taught not to express anger, and this feeling gives way to a more general hostility, which emphasizes the disunity and disharmony between people. Such hostility keeps the person continuously producing the strong chemicals that are needed to convey anger quickly and directly. This produces physiological stressors for the body. Also, when a person lacks awareness about these hostile feelings, a barrier is imposed to healing the broken relationship between the self and the other person.

Similarly, feelings of hopelessness and helplessness that are sustained over time deplete the body of energy and resources for positive adaptation. Seligman (1994), for example, argues that girls in our American culture learn helplessness and, therefore, become depressed more frequently than do boys. Physiological responses such as the reduction of endorphins and other neurotransmitter substances associated with feeling good and being happy may result from continued frustration in meeting one's goals. Frustration results when a person meets with resistance along life's journey. The field of endocrinology is just beginning to map the locations and functions of these neurotransmitter substances and their effects on health and healing (Dossey, Keegan, Guzzetta, & Kolkmeier, 1988). As these maps and methods are revealed, people will have even more resources for understanding themselves in relation to others. This type of understanding will contribute to awareness and healing.

Social and cultural belief systems often prevent human beings from acknowledging honestly and openly how they feel and what they want. Consequently, discomfort and disease often occur as the body eventually succumbs to its own protective responses related to these strong feelings. Lack of awareness about the close relationship between emotions and physiologic response prevents us from healing. This lack of awareness itself is a barrier to healing and living in harmony with the environment. A person living between cultures, such as the Korean wife of an American businessman, may suffer from Kwa-Byung or fire illness because she is trying to accommodate the expectations of two cultures (Kim, 1993). Her dominant Korean culture emphasizes the importance of hiding bad or negative feelings, while the American culture admonishes her to *let it all hang out* and express herself. Without awareness of the impact of cultural expectations and conflicts between competing cultures, the Korean-American wife may suffer from physical and emotional illnesses because this lack of awareness acts as an impediment to full expression of the human healing potential.

Social Conditions

Specific social conditions contribute to the lack of awareness about the human mind-body connection. Social isolation and lack of education prevent many individuals from understanding the relationship between what they feel and how their bodies respond to demands from the environment. These social conditions lead to feelings of disconnectedness, which, according to Cassell (1976), result in illness or sickness. Children who are isolated from other children have no frame of reference when they experience fear in abusive relationships with parents. When these same parents, upon whom the children's very lives depend, threaten to withhold necessities such as food or love if the children express fear of pain when threatened with a beating, the children fragment these experiences. Such fragmentation interferes with the development of awareness essential for healing and health. Fragmentation of lived experience and disconnection from the nurturance of other human beings represent enormous barriers to healing. When these barriers are experienced at an early age, they further obstruct the child from pursuing a healing lifestyle that includes connecting with nurturing others.

Parents who are uneducated and unable to socialize with other parents fail to learn how to recognize and accept the variety of feelings that are normal to have in response to raising children. Fearful of these feelings, they may strike out at the children, blaming them for causing the parents to be out of control. Similarly, single parents who have no partners with whom to discuss feelings and uncertainties may experience extraordinary pressure in raising children alone. The support of social relationships is essential to feeling connected, learning what is socially acceptable behavior, and thus maintaining health. Social isolation forms an impediment to the very network of interpersonal relationships that support awareness and healing.

Social Institutions

Established social institutions that were created to contribute to the health and welfare of people at times become barriers to healing. Among such institutions are the public schools, governmental agencies, and hospitals. Such institutions become ends in themselves when their focuses are narrow rather than comprehensive, and they become mired in bureaucratic details. A good example is the forced separation between church and state as played out in the ban on prayer in schools. Despite research findings that provide evidence for a correlation between prayer and healing (Dossey, 1993), defenders of the United States Constitution demand that the rights of atheists, although a minority in America, should be the rule in public schools. The consequences in terms of children's and communities' health are rarely discussed. The United States Constitution and the agencies constructed to support it are abused when they are cast as barricades to the freedom of living in healing relationships.

A political economy approach to health care in America also stands as a barrier to healing. Marginalized groups, those who fall outside the privileged majority of citizens, such as women, physically disabled persons, ethnic minorities, and the aging, frequently receive less-than-adequate health care services (Lupton, 1994). The institution of medicine promotes such inequalities by refusing to allocate adequate resources to disadvantaged citizens who cannot contribute to the American economic system.

Patterns of Behavior

Several patterns of human behaviors interfere with the development of awareness that is essential to healing. These behaviors may be habits or rituals that originally serve a purpose such as reducing anxiety within the person. Without conscious awareness of the purpose they are serving and a willingness to consider other alternatives, these patterns of behavior become self-destructive. Such behaviors include the use and eventual abuse of drugs such as alcohol and nicotine, early and promiscuous sexual intimacy, irresponsible and inappropriate use of motor vehicles, and sedentary lifestyles. Each of these behaviors may initially enhance a person's experience, as is often the case with moderate use of alcohol. However, when these behaviors begin to form patterns of responses that prevent the person from being aware of how life experiences contribute to or detract from healing and health, they no longer play a positive role in the human health experience. Habits that may originate in ways that expand consciousness may quickly turn to rituals that deprive one of full conscious awareness.

High-risk behaviors such as the abuse of chemicals, sexual experimentation, and inappropriate use of motor vehicles usually begin in adolescence before adult patterns of behaviors are established (Crockett & Petersen, 1993). Adolescence is a time of transition from the developmental tasks of childhood to the privileges and responsibilities of adulthood. Experimentation with mind-expanding activities can easily lead to derailment when self-control is not imposed. The abuse of adult privileges becomes a prison for developing healing awareness. The high-risk behaviors of adolescents often lead to the dulling of sensations and conscious awareness through accidental misuse and permanent injury associated with this misuse. Such high-risk behaviors are usually prompted by a need for attention and a need to cease dependence on parents or other adults. The need to be noticed and valued may not be met through more healthy and nurturing relationships; thus the adolescent seeks a quick fix, often with dire consequences.

Patterns of high-risk behavior can consume so much energy that the person is prevented from consciously understanding the many dimensions and consequences of the behavior. Engaging in high-risk behaviors may involve the denial that detrimental consequences could occur or beliefs about being omnipotent. This latter type of belief is translated into thinking that negative outcomes could happen only to somebody else.

BARRIERS TO HEALING

Cooper states that "healing activities have always formed the basis of nursing practice" (1990, p. 166) and she asserts that the 1980s could be referred to as the era of the wound. Cooper notes that much has been learned by nurses about what affects the healing of physical wounds. For example, some factors that promote healing include the availability of oxygen to injured tissues, the lack of other injuries, the positive nutritional status of the individual, the patient's feeling of safety, the control of pain, the support and nearness of loved ones, and an environment that is not cold. These factors create a setting in which healing is better than when such conditions do not exist. Cooper adds, "Not unlike a waterfall, healing is a cascading process composed of multiple small goal-directed events that combine and result in the creation of something more complex and energy rich than any one component considered by itself" (p. 170). This view of healing underscores the holistic nature of the process. What has been learned by nurses about the healing of physical wounds points once again to the importance of the environment (oxygen, nutrition, safety, and temperature) and the support of personal relationships.

Because awareness is essential to the process of healing, barriers to self-awareness also become barriers to healing. The outcomes of strong feelings that are not acknowledged and expressed openly and directly by people prevent those people from healing the discomfort and disharmony in their lives. In the vignette of Harriet and Jonathan, unacceptable feelings were not acknowledged by Harriet and consequently led to damage and discomfort in her gastrointestinal system. The more she ignored these feelings, the farther she got from healing the physical symptoms and the disruptions in her interpersonal relationships.

Cimprich (1992) notes that the person who seeks health care needs to pay a lot of attention to many things at a time when the capacity to pay attention may be diminished due to disease, perceived vulnerability, or fatigue. She adds that when people enter health care facilities they may be unfamiliar with the use of language and routines and be overwhelmed by a vast amount of complex information. When demands on attention are complex and prolonged, the people may become tired and unable to focus attention or apply relevant information to themselves. Cimprich suggests that a supportive environment in which people can make choices and retain some power for self-determination can offset the barriers to awareness that are created with information overload or attentional fatigue.

Mind-Body Communication

Recent research into the intricacies of brain structure and chemistry provides fascinating explanations of the communication that takes place between the mind and the body. Studies of the brain and spinal cord that have been made possible by modern technologies such as surgery, CAT scans, and magnetic resonance imaging (MRI) have led to a comprehensive mapping of the functions of various components of the nervous system and the way in which information is communicated within this system. Disorders that were once a mystery and viewed as hopeless have relented to new interventions in rehabilitation.

Candace Pert (1987), a biochemist, is one of the first researchers to study chemical messengers within the human body. These chemicals, known as neuropeptides, and the cells that act as receptors of them, form an information network that links the mind and body together intimately. Neuropeptides may enter the body from an external source as medicines or they may be produced and released within the body as endorphins and hormones. The cells that receive these chemicals, the receptors, form the biochemical structure basic to human emotions. Neuropeptides, according to Pert, "bring us to a state of consciousness and to alterations in those states" (p. 15). Thus, there is mounting evidence of the delicate communication that contributes to the natural healing that occurs within the human body-mind. Based on her work in biochemistry, Pert demonstrates that the mind consists of information that flows throughout all parts of the body by way of a complex network. The mind is not confined just to the brain and nervous system. People can become more aware of the intricacies of this information flow and the part the mind plays in healing through conscious awareness and control of breathing. Pert (1990) questions whether the mind is in the brain. She discusses the role of opiate receptors and endorphins as chemicals that mediate the subjective experience of pain.

She cites the examples of yogis who train themselves not to experience pain and women in labor who do not become overwhelmed by the perception of pain. In both examples, the individual consciously controls these internal responses through focused breathing.

Rene Dubos (1990), who is in his late 70s, describes three occasions during his life when he almost died. As a scientist and philosopher, he has some profound things to say about the nature of healing. He asserts that the most important idea about human healing is that whatever happens to people is based on deliberate choices that reflect beliefs about the future. He adds that adapting to a complex and changing environment is not the mere unfolding of genetics through a process of predictable development but takes place through "awareness, motivation, free will, and ability to anticipate the future" (p. 143). Healing depends on information communicated between the mind and the body. Healing also depends on information communicated between people.

Social Relationships

Formal and informal relationships between people can either facilitate or hinder the healing process. As noted previously, social conditions of isolation prevent the development of awareness among people. By the same token, lack of social contact or social support can also interrupt the healing process. David Spiegel, a psychiatrist at Stanford University, recently found that women with serious breast cancer who participated in a support group lived twice as long as women who did not participate in such a group (Graham, 1992). The women in the support group were encouraged to share the full range of feelings they experienced about their illness and treatments. These women found that the process of open sharing increased their awareness of being alive and they experienced healing even though the disease itself was not cured. Participating in informal discussions with others who were ill enabled these women to reflect on the meaning and purpose of their lives. They learned much about making choices about living. The experience of being connected through a social support network expresses the importance of human relationships to the healing process. A harmony between the individuals in this network exemplifies healing in spite of the presence of physical disease.

Self-awareness, self-care, and self-direction facilitate healing. In contrast, preventing persons from participating in their health care decisions and activities retards the healing process. When people are taken care of by well-meaning others, they often develop a type of hopeless or helpless dependency that interrupts their natural striving for self-actualization. Recent research shows that when people participate in health care decisions and health care activities, this participation increases the competence of their immune systems, decreases blood pressure, and diminishes the sensation of pain (Gordon, 1992). All of these factors work together to promote the integration of people with their environments. Regardless of the illness or injury, awareness of one's intrinsic as well as extrinsic resources contributes positively to the process of healing.

Lifestyle

There are many modern lifestyles that act as barriers to the natural healing processes characteristic of human beings. These include the fast pace of living on schedules and feeling the need to beat the clock in meeting self- or other-imposed deadlines. Closely associated with this behavior is the perception that to be loved and valued by family and society, a person must live up to the expectations imposed by those important others. Consequently, many people develop habits and routines that result in living out another person's agenda rather than being self-directed. Many theories about dysfunctional families and co-dependent partners testify to the destructive pathways followed by persons living these types of unhealthy lifestyles.

Nurses, as healers, should be aware of their vulnerability to getting caught up in a lifestyle that robs them of energy and creativity. Heinrich and Killeen (1993) assert that nurses need to learn how to take better care of themselves. They wrote a special fable for nurses and called it *The Gift*. It's a delightful story about the Spirit of Cheer and Harmony, whose job is to bring gifts to special people — in this case, to the Generous People, the nurses who give to others. The gift turns out to be a small box wrapped in shiny paper with a small message tucked inside that says, *take a day for yourself.* One nurse in the fable, Donata, refused to take the gift seriously, thinking that she had to do just one more thing to help her patient. However, the demands of constantly giving to others caught up with Donata and she finally decided to use her gift by spending a day with a child. Donata learned how much enjoyment she had in receiving the gift. The Spirit of Cheer and Harmony reminds nurses that in order to provide the healing touch to a client, the nurse must first nurture the self. The authors of the fable add that without humor and joy, there is no healing. This example shows once more the importance of a mutuality in living. Healing follows a dynamic and reciprocal process of giving and receiving between people and the environment.

AWARENESS OF BARRIERS

There are many similarities in the barriers to awareness and the barriers to healing because awareness and healing are both processes inherent in human living. Stuart, Deckro, and Mandle (1989) view health as the interaction between individuals and their environments. Healing requires the individual to examine the challenge and opportunity in illness; the opportunity in illness is to look at life with a renewed sense of meaning and purpose. Becoming aware of those things that interfere with our full awareness and its relationship to healing is a first step in altering the course of injury, illness, and discomfort. This awareness is improved as persons learn to know themselves more fully.

Learning to know the self is an act of taking responsibility and it is powerful (Hay, 1991). Much of our mental activity takes place outside our awareness and is a storehouse for creative potential (Harman & Rheingold, 1984). When we focus on our problems and limitations, we firmly establish our greatest barrier to healing. Altering our consiousness through relaxation and other mind-opening and freeing exercises can radically reduce the number of barriers we experience. Mental phenomena of personal knowledge and intuition contribute to self-understanding and are the focus of chapter 6. Exercises in chapter 8 give specific directions about how to increase self-awareness and enhance healing potentials.

References

Cassell, E. J. (1976). *The healer's art*. Philadelphia: J. B. Lippincott Company.

Cimprich, B. (1992). A theoretical perspective on attention and patient education. *Advances in Nursing Science, 14* (3), 39–51.

Cooper, D. M. (1990). Optimizing wound healing: A practice within nursing's domain. *Nursing Clinics of North America, 25* (1), 165–180.

Crockett, L. J., & Petersen, A. C. (1993). Adolescent development: Health risks and opportunities for health promotion. In S. G. Millstein, A. C. Petersen, & E. O. Nightingale, *Promoting the health of adolescents* (pp. 13–37). New York: Oxford University Press.

Dossey, B. M., Keegan, L., Guzzetta, C. E., & Kolkmeier, L. G. (1988). *Holistic nursing: A handbook for practice*. Rockville, MD: Aspen Publishers, Inc.

Dossey, L. (1993). Health and prayer: The power of paradox and mystery. *Noetic Sciences Review, 28*, 22–25.

Dubos, R. (1990). Self-healing: A personal history. In R. Ornstein & C. Sencionis (Eds.), *The healing brain: A scientific reader* (pp. 135–146). New York: The Guilford Press.

Faber, M. D. (1981). *Culture and consciousness*. New York: Human Sciences Press.

Goldberg, P. (1983). *The intuitive edge*. Los Angeles: Jeremy P. Tarcher, Inc.

Gordon, J. S. (1992). Healing from within. In Educational Publishing Department, *Healing and the mind with Bill Moyers: A viewer's guide* (pp. 8–9). *Institute of Noetic Sciences Bulletin, 7* (4).

Graham, B. (1992). Wounded healers. In Educational Publishing Department, *Healing and the mind with Bill Moyers: A viewer's guide* (pp. 12–13). *Institute of Noetic Sciences Bulletin, 7* (4).

Harman, W., & Rheingold, H. (1984). *Higher creativity*. Los Angeles: Jeremy P. Tarcher, Inc.

Hay, L. L. (1991). *The power is within you*. Carson, CA: Hay House, Inc.

Heinrich, K., & Killeen, M. E. (1993). The gentle art of nurturing yourself. *American Journal of Nursing, 93* (10), 41–44.

Kim, S. (1993). *Ethnic identity, role integration, quality of life, and mental health in Korean American women*. Unpublished doctoral dissertation, The University of Texas at Austin.

Lupton, D. (1994). *Medicine as culture: Illness, disease, and the body in western societies*. Thousand Oaks, CA: Sage Publications.

Pert, C. (1987). Neuropeptides: The emotions and body-mind. *Noetic Sciences Review*, Spring, 13–18.

Pert, C. (1990). The wisdom of the receptors: Neuropeptides, the emotions, and body-mind. In R. Ornstein & C. Swencionis (Eds.), *The healing brain: A scientific reader* (pp. 147–158). New York: The Guilford Press.

Rossi, E. L., & Cheek, D. B. (1988). *Mind-body therapy: Ideodynamic healing in hypnosis.* New York: W. W. Norton & Company.

Seligman, M. E. P. (1994). *What you can change and what you can't.* New York: Alfred A. Knopf.

Selye, H. (1956/1976). *The stress of life.* New York: McGraw-Hill.

Stuart, E. M., Deckro, J. P., & Mandle, C. L. (1989). Spirituality in health and healing: A clinical program. *Holistic Nursing Practice, 3* (3), 35–46.

Suggested Reading

Geary, P. A., & Hawkins, J. W. (1992). The ritual of healing. *Healthcare Trends & Transition, 3* (3), 8–10.

4 | AESTHETICS AND THE HEALING ENVIRONMENT

> *Let every pupil in training and every graduate nurse take heed that their broader usefulness can only come when they grasp fully the conditions that belong to the sick-room, conditions constantly changing and never met by the mere administration of drugs or giving of a bath. To grasp the whole situation and meet it without obtrusiveness or sentimental nonsense is the gift of woman more than man, but among women the gift varies and is susceptible of cultivation.*
>
> E. D. Ferguson, 1901

Mindy and Beverly

Mindy was 16 years old when she brought Beverly, the school nurse, a delicate pastel drawing of a small mouse with huge ears, standing timidly by an enormous strawberry plant. Mindy weighed only 76 pounds and in her mind's eye the skinny kid diagnosed with anorexia nervosa was still horribly obese. When she surveyed her body, Mindy found nothing that she thought was beautiful, but when asked to draw something of beauty, a shy mouse with big ears and a plant bearing a juicy red strawberry came quickly to her mind. The nurse kept the picture and over several months explored with Mindy the deeper meaning and significance of these symbols of beauty.

Each week when Mindy came to Beverly's office, she was dressed neatly in clean jeans and a big shirt. Her hair was never out of place and although she never wore makeup, Mindy's skin was creamy and clear. In spite of her obvious attention to hygiene and neatness, there was an overwhelming heaviness and sadness in the way she carried her tiny frame. She walked slowly and sank deeply into the sofa when she sat down.

Mindy had been losing weight steadily for close to a year before her mother and sister finally persuaded her to visit the doctor. Mindy had two younger sisters who enjoyed experimenting with makeup, wearing each other's clothes to expand their wardrobes, and talking incessantly on the phone. In contrast, Mindy had adopted a role of the wiser, if sadder, older sister, conscientious about her grades and diligent in following the rules set by parents and teachers. She often cooked for the family, carefully measuring and weighing the ingredients of the various recipes she tried. But when dinner was served, Mindy stared blankly at her plate, merely picking at pieces of food and moving them around with her fork to make it look as if she had eaten.

It was difficult for Mindy to talk about herself. More often than not she would answer questions about herself quickly, then add information about one of her sisters or her mother. Her sense of self-worth and identity were almost nonexistent. But when Beverly asked her to draw a picture of how she felt, Mindy created beautiful symbolic messages of her faint presence in a bewildering and gigantic world. Her picture of the mouse with the huge ears symbolized her belief that she should stay out of sight, listening and rarely squeaking. She was to be seen but not heard. She longed for nourishment and one day shortly after sharing her drawing of the mouse with Beverly,

Mindy brought a salad plate full of strawberries with her and suggested that Beverly share the snack with her. This event was a turning point in the healing relationship between Mindy and her nurse.

Mindy's nurse, Beverly, portrays the application of aesthetics to the process of healing. By encouraging Mindy to draw something beautiful, Beverly was able to help Mindy become aware of what was beautiful and meaningful in her inner world of wisdom. She had been unable to stimulate this awareness by talking and providing emotional support. By dealing directly with Mindy's perceptive or intuitive awareness, Beverly was then able to work with Mindy's skill and interpretation to build the types of awareness she needed to heal her broken body and the dissatisfying relationships with her family.

AESTHETICS

Aesthetics refers to the sense of beauty or the study of what is beautiful. Knowledge of aesthetics can be used to promote healing. The term *aesthetics* is derived from the Greek *aistheta* meaning to feel. It refers to those things apprehended through the senses and through language. In the English language, the word *aesthetic* eventually became synonymous with thinking about the arts, whose forms and structures were taken in through the senses, and the resulting feelings about these experiences (Shipley, 1945). The word *anesthetic* became a related term used by medical science to refer to the act of removing sensation or feeling in part of the body.

Philosophers throughout the ages have grappled with the objective and subjective nature of what is pleasing to the senses. According to Plato, there is an Absolute Beauty that transcends individual forms of beauty and is an idea worthy of contemplation. In Plato's view, beauty transcends time and space, and manifests itself in the harmony that contains the parts within the whole (Dieckmann, 1973). It is the notion that beauty is an idea of connection and harmony that makes the discussion of aesthetics appropriate to an understanding of the healing process.

Aesthetic knowledge in nursing has until recently been part of the informal education of nurses. The art of nursing is recognized as part of the rich heritage of the discipline, yet it has escaped formal scrutiny by the majority of nurse scientists. Carper (1978) identified aesthetic knowledge as one of four fundamental patterns of greatest importance to nursing. In her review of the meaning of aesthetics, Carper discusses perception, in contrast to recognition, as the quality of action that leads to a synthesis of means and ends. It is in this creative synthesis that the art of healing is expressed. Carper adds that this pattern of knowing is expressed through empathy and reflects an awareness of the unique subjective experience of the client.

Aesthetics, as a way of knowing in nursing, is exemplified in the example of Beverly, the nurse in the vignette about Mindy. Beverly felt empathy toward her client but was unable to prompt a cognitive recognition from Mindy about what was troubling her. However, by respecting the unique and subjective experience that was locked inside Mindy, Beverly was able to assist Mindy with directly connecting her inner world of confusion and pain to an outward expression that could be seen and experienced through her senses. The drawing of a caricature of a mouse was connected to symbolic meaning that Mindy found difficult to describe directly with words. The picture communicated to others how insignificant Mindy felt in the world of other people, but within herself the little mouse with huge ears was a creature of beauty.

As a culture, Americans probably associate healing more with the anesthetics used during surgery or dental work to save us from painful stimuli than with aesthetics or paying attention to what is beautiful around us. Learning to see the patterns of beauty and harmony in nature can facilitate an awareness of healing. Just as people recovering from anesthesia breathe more easily and are less nauseous when they are encouraged to look around the room and get a sense of unity with the environment rather than to look down only at the floor, so too do people in search of healing progress by considering the aesthetics of the environment as a whole rather than concentrating on the brokenness of their individual parts in it.

The quotation from Ferguson at the beginning of this chapter expresses the understanding that nurses have of the importance of the context in which healing takes place. The administration of technical procedures alone does not result in healing. It is the artful way in which such procedures are done that enhances the healing process and focuses on the essential component of interpersonal relationships. In the vignette about Mindy, the nurse facilitated the healing of Mindy's disharmony by tapping into her symbolic expression of her fears. What was difficult for Mindy to put into words was portrayed emphatically through her drawings. These drawings reflected her personal view of the world and how she fit into it as an insignificant little rodent. The picture she carried around of herself was difficult to articulate in words, but the direct expression of her drawing was unmistakably clear.

Medical and nursing sciences have assembled an impressive number of facts and theoretical models that help in understanding processes of illness and healing. Only recently have the results of systematic investigation validated what nurses have known for centuries: aesthetics are essential to the context of healing. Because people experience their environments through the senses of sight, smell, sound, taste, and touch, each of these senses can be addressed when creating a healing environment. The aesthetic qualities of the healing relationship are based on beliefs of wholeness, harmony, and beauty that are unique to each healing encounter. They reflect many of the philosophies reviewed in chapter 2. The outcomes of healing represent the creative perceptions of re-establishing wholeness. These outcomes affect expansion of cognitive, intuitive, and transcendent awareness.

THE HEALING ENVIRONMENT

The sensations of humans connect them with their environments. The human capacity for sight, sound, smell, taste, and touch are well known. Each contributes a richness to the feelings of being whole and healthy. These connections can promote the experience of harmony and healing or that of disharmony and disease. The difference in outcomes depends on the specific stimuli and the perception or interpretation of those stimuli to the individual. When people are ill, the sensations may be dulled and interfere with the healing process. Promoting the healing process requires that we enhance the positive experiences of all the sensations. Aesthetic knowledge can be applied to enhance the healing of persons by acknowledging how one's environment is perceived by an individual through all the senses. This can be accomplished through an empathic nurse-client relationship.

Sight

Visual sensation provides people with much important information about the world. How the environment looks to the individual depends on the person's perception of visual stimuli and influences how the environment facilitates or impedes the process of healing. Thus, environments can be constructed or modified to promote healing. For example, having personal possessions such as a clock and a picture of one's family on the bedside table of a hospitalized client contributes positively to a healing environment by providing positive visual stimuli. Much of what human beings know and understand about the world comes into conscious awareness through the sensation of sight. Vision is the most well-developed sensation of human beings and the visual cortex constitutes a fairly large portion of the cerebral structure of the brain (Zeki, 1993). The sensation of sight provides information to the human mind about an ever-changing environment with which the person seeks harmony. The ability to differentiate colors, shapes, textures, and distances are but a few examples of the exquisite abilities afforded the human species through the experience of sight. When sight is interrupted, a person's experience of the environment is compromised until another of the major senses takes over. When harmony between a person and the environment is disrupted, visualization through real or imagined images holds promise as a vehicle for healing.

Visualization and Imagery   Images are mental representations of objects seen or imagined (Zahourek, 1988). Visual images occur spontaneously or they may be induced by suggestion. They have been used both to torment and to heal people throughout recorded history. In recent years, the study of mental imagery or visualization has gained popularity as a therapeutic technique in disciplines of psychology, education, and nursing. Many variations in the technique are seen from the use of mental images to cure individuals with phobias to the use of visualization to promote healing after myocardial infarction, and to help sports teams improve their winning records.

A growing number of research studies in nursing provide evidence of the healing powers of stimulating mental imagery in children, adults, and the elderly. Visualization and imagery have been used in conjunction with other therapeutic strategies such as progressive relaxation to control pain and anxiety. They have also been used with Therapeutic Touch, which will be discussed in more detail later in this chapter, to provide healing energy to physical wounds. The technique of visualization and imagery has been used with both individual clients and groups (Simonton & Henson, 1992).

In the context of a healing relationship, visualization or imagery is generally guided by one person for the benefit of altering the experience of pain or illness in another person. The guide helps the client to gain access to an inner vision or way of seeing. Through suggestion, various perceptions may be introduced into the client's imagination. The guide generally reinforces the person's ability to control and change images as desired. Also, the guide reinforces that this ability to control the imagination and visualize a desirable outcome is a powerful healing resource of the client.

Including visualization and imagery as a noninvasive intervention demonstrates the application of aesthetic knowledge in healing. It is one way of including a rich resource that the client has within but may need assistance in realizing. Some of the exercises in chapter 8 illustrate the use of imagery in healing and in increasing conscious awareness of both healer and healee. Imagery interventions can include suggesting specific visualizations such as places where an individual has previously been and can imagine through a memorable experience. Such interventions can include the suggestion of symbolic visions such as the opening of a rosebud, the stretching of roots underground, or the movement of blood through an artery or vein. Guided imagery used in conjunction with keeping a diary of images and dreams can facilitate conscious awareness that facilitates healing.

Hallucinations   The sensation of visual images can be debilitating as well as healing. Hallucinations illustrate the power of images to alter a person's experience of the environment. They are perceptions that occur without a visual stimulus from the environment and are generally distortions of real objects (Zeki,

1993). Hallucinations are similar to dreams. The sensations that accompany them are very real to the person who experiences them. Working directly with a person's visual sensation, whether it be a direct response to a visual stimulus from the external environment or a covert response to something happening internally, provides another avenue for healing. Perlaky (1994) describes the creative response of a granddaughter-in-law to her 81-year-old grandfather's problems with Alzheimer's disease. The man experienced repeated hallucinations of flying polar bears. Visiting nurses had attempted to no avail to orient the man to reality by insisting that there were no such things as flying polar bears, so they could not possibly be hurting him. Yet the hallucinations persisted and the grandfather became increasingly distressed. His granddaughter-in-law understood that his perception of the flying polar bears was real to him, so she sought a solution to his problem of distress. She covered a spray can with paper on which she had drawn flying polar bears. She brought the can into his bedroom and as he described where the bothersome creatures were, she sprayed with sincerity. The hallucinations stopped at once and never reappeared.

Sound

The environment produces a wide variety of auditory stimuli in the form of sounds and noises. Noise pollution is now recognized as a common health hazard leading to poor productivity and actual physical damage in people with repeated exposure to loud and irritating sounds (Keegan, 1988a). Many physiological alterations such as changes in blood pressure and respiration have been associated with noise levels in the environment. Mechanical noises that are dissonant disrupt the healing process, whereas harmonic sounds promote healing. An environment where sound is pleasing and enjoyable allows a person to relax and feel a unity that would not be experienced in a setting where noises jolt and unsettle the person.

Suggestion Verbal messages given with medical treatments have been shown to alter the physiological responses of patients. This has been described as the placebo effect and is a legitimate way to mobilize a person's internal self-healing (Sobel, 1990).

Many examples illustrate the power of suggestion in altering blood pressure and blood flow, and in controlling pain. This strategy has also been used extensively with visualization and imagery in patients with cancer to trigger the body's immune system (Simonton, Matthews-Simonton, & Creighton, 1978; Simonton & Henson, 1992).

Music   Nurse researchers have shown that music decreases the perception of pain in some people. Schorr (1993) conducted an exploratory study of 30 women who had arthritis and who ranged in age from 31 to 81 years. The purpose of her study was to investigate the use of music as an intervention to alter the perception of pain in these women. Each of the subjects selected her favorite type of music to listen to while maintaining a comfortable position for a period of 20 minutes. Indicators of pain were recorded prior to the intervention, at the conclusion of 20 minutes of listening to the self-selected music, and at another interval of 2 hours. Schorr found statistically significant differences in the subjects' perceptions of pain between the three time periods. As time went on, the subjects' perceptions of pain associated with their arthritic conditions decreased. Schorr concluded that this study provides support for the use of music as a healing strategy that is appropriate for women with rheumatoid arthritis. Music, according to Schorr, is a way for the nurse healer to connect in an authentic and noninvasive way with a client whose movement within the environment is limited by the perception of pain. Through the use of music, barriers to conscious awareness that would otherwise limit the person's experience are overcome. The person whose previous awareness focused on limitation and inabilities becomes transformed into imagining possibilities of new ways to interact and feel more in harmony with the environment.

In a review of the literature concerning the effects of music on pain, Whipple and Glynn (1992) noted that nurses have traditionally used music and other noninvasive techniques to assist clients in controlling pain. Music is a way to help a person attend to pleasant rather than unpleasant sensations. Researchers have documented the effects of music on physiological responses such as decreases in blood pressure in persons with coronary disease and those undergoing surgery. Likewise, music has been associated with decreased discomfort among women in labor and in the perception of pain experienced by persons with cancer. The type of music that is effective in altering physiological responses to pain and illness may be unique to each individual. Thus, it is the aesthetic application of these findings to the healing relationship between nurse and client that is essential to the outcome.

The sensation of hearing is of utmost importance in understanding the communication between the conscious and unconscious awareness of a person. Rossi and Cheek (1988) maintain that there is a continuous process of communication between the external environment and a person's unconscious mind at all times. They provide many examples of how a person undergoing surgery with complete loss of sensation due to anesthesia can hear conversations in the operating room. The unconscious mind hears the conversation literally but because the person is not fully conscious and aware of the context for the words spoken, may interpret the words incorrectly. Consequently, persons who were expected to have a normal postoperative recovery suddenly experienced unexplained hemorrhaging or other complications that disrupted the process of healing. Hypnotic suggestion bypasses the usual alert awareness associated with hearing and allows direct access to the hearing unconscious mind. These examples illustrate the importance of sound in the healing process.

Smell

The sensation of smell is essential to survival. The instincts to eat and to engage in sexual activity for reproduction are based on an intact sense of smell (Poppel, 1988). Although less well-developed than in other mammals, the sense of smell contributes to the ongoing evolution of human beings. Olfactory sensation also is recognized as a path to enjoying life and represents a dimension of aesthetic knowledge. Scents are recognized in variations of sweet, sour, pungent, and so forth. Some are associated with warm and healing experiences such as the aroma of freshly baked bread, herbal tea, or steaming broth. Others are associated with sexual excitement as seen in the myriad products sold to promote romance, intimacy, and success in the American culture. Still others conjure up disgust and are associated with decay and destruction.

Odors that indicate decay and destruction act as barriers to both awareness and healing. In a hospital setting, for instance, lack of attention to bathroom odors may distract an individual from resting and feeling at harmony with the environment. Similarly, a client being visited by a friend, or even a nurse or other health care provider, who is wearing strong perfume or cologne may feel nauseous. This aroma can interfere with the healing process. Some smells that typically evoke a positive response in the well person may suddenly be perceived as detrimental to the person who feels ill.

Recent research provides evidence that human beings, like many other mammals, have a sensory structure in the nose known as the vomeronasal organ (VNO). The purpose of this organ is to detect chemical cues associated with sexual behaviors. The VNO occupies a very small place on either side of the nasal septum and can be seen on visual inspection of the human nose (Taylor, 1994). Little else is known and understood about the function these small organs play in mediating behavior. However, this research suggests that there are factors within the environment that influence human behavior without our conscious awareness of them. These tiny organs may even play an important part in the intuitive knowledge nurses develop about their critically ill patients.

In healing, the sense of smell provides an avenue for connecting the ill or distressed person with a harmonious environment or relationship. Fresh flowers and plants have long been recognized as gifts of cheer for the ill and infirm, not only for the aesthetic quality of visual experience but also for their refreshing and stimulating aromas. Hot meals, especially those that include soup and broth with rich, tempting smells, have also been associated with healing and strength. These aromas lead directly to healing responses such as relaxation within the body. Symbolically, these smells may suggest a time and/or place when the person was safe and happy. Such aromas are typically associated with a message of being cared for or about. The olfactory sensation may even give rise to harmonious visual images that also contribute to the healing process.

A healing environment contains aromas that are pleasing and support feelings of harmony. Removing odors that are offensive and sickening was advocated in the early writings of Florence Nightingale in the mid-1800s. She advised nurses to air the room of a patient with air from outside, ridding it of odors such as gas, paint, chimney smoke, and "the current of sewer air from an ill-placed sink" (Nightingale, 1946, p. 12). She added that "a slop-pail should never be brought into a sick room" (p. 14). Nightingale, credited as the nurse who began the first formal and systematic education of nurses, was adamant about the necessity for a clean and organized environment for the sick. She further recognized that given all of these essential components of a healing environment, the process of nursing a patient back to health was an art that could not be learned by reading rules from a textbook.

Taste

Nutrition has long been associated with the healing process because of its biochemical foundation for growth and repair of tissues (Cooper, 1990). The art of nursing includes the presentation of food and fluids to patients recovering from disease and injury. It is well-known that appetite is affected by illness and the return of appetite is easily identified as an indicator of recovery. Persons who are ill often report that foods they usually like no longer taste good and when they are on the mend, they state that familiar foods taste unusually good. The sensation of taste is mediated to some extent by the perception that food is good for us and certain foods take on added meaning related to associating them with particular positive events such as holidays.

Florence Nightingale had plenty to say about the nutrition of the sick and the aesthetic presentation of food to the patient as well. She said, "Let the food come at the right time, and be taken away, eaten or uneaten, at the right time; but never let a patient have 'something always standing' by him, if you don't wish to disgust him of everything" (Nightingale, 1946, p. 37). She understood the importance of adequate nutrition for healing, but she also was guiding healers to consider what food the patient liked and when it would be best for him to consume it. Since Nightingale's time, much has been learned about the role of nutrition in disease as well as in healing. Recently new facts are being established about the effects of food on the mind of a person. Foods may have direct effects on the release of neurotransmitters in the body and, therefore, affect human consciousness and awareness (Wurtman, 1990). Nutrition plays a part not only in effecting direct physiological changes within the person but influences the mental activity and awareness of the person as well.

One aspect of the relationship between the sense of taste and the conscious awareness of the person is the connection between the actual chemical-nutritional value of the food and its presentation. The same food presented in an aesthetically pleasing way evokes a more positive emotional and physiological response than it does if presented straight from a box or can. Early nursing education in this country emphasized the importance of the patient's meal tray in the hospital and in the home. Adding a fresh flower, a cheerful message on a card, a small candle, or a brightly colored napkin to the tray were a few of the suggestions for cheering up an acutely ill or convalescing patient (Wood, 1926). The size of the tray relative to the portion of food presented was also emphasized as an important detail to consider in promoting a healing environment.

The meaning of food and eating to the individual relates to the healing process. The infant's earliest perception of the environment includes sensations of eating and physical, social contact. Over time, the individual collects a variety of experiences that associate food and eating with positive or negative feelings. Many of a family's rituals about mealtime are closely connected with emotions that contribute to feeling loved and healthy. On the other hand, punishment is sometimes meted out to children by forcing them to eat food that is not appealing or through abusive behaviors involving the mouth.

Touch

The sensation of touch and its relationship to the healing arts can be traced to the ancient ritual of the laying on of hands. There is a transfer of energy between people when one person literally touches another. The energy transfer can have a positive or negative effect on the person being touched, depending on the intention of the person initiating the touch. For example, a woman who receives a gentle stroking of her upper arm as an expression of affection from her husband experiences a positive transfer of energy whereas another woman who receives a rough grasp and violent jerking at the hand of her husband experiences a negative transfer of energy. A similar phenomenon of positive energy transfer occurs in the affective domain when people report that the action of another person touched them, which means that the person's behavior had a positive effect on them. Touch, then, is another resource to be implemented in the art of healing. A healing touch may be delivered in the form of body massage, applying pressure, bathing the body, combing or brushing the hair, dressing a wound, or rocking and caressing a person.

The skin is the largest sensory organ of the body, permitting a wide array of information from the environment to enter into the inner awareness of the person. As a sensory organ, the skin communicates a variety of sensations to the person living inside it. Perception, again, plays an important part in mediating the stimuli from the external environment to the awareness in the conscious mind of the person. The meaning of touch to a client may be tied to positive or negative experiences in the past and the nurse healer should never touch a client without first seeking and obtaining permission. For those individuals who have been traumatized by abusive touch in intimate relationships with parents or lovers, physical contact between nurse and client may be grossly misunderstood. The types of healing touch presented here are examples of positive interventions that can be used when touch is perceived as positive.

Massage   As early as the fifth century B.C., Hippocrates, the Greek known as the father of medicine, asserted that a person who wanted to provide healing therapies should learn how to massage (Kaslof, 1978). Over the centuries, various techniques originating in China, Japan, Sweden, and several other European countries made their way to America. Today at least four basic techniques may be identified in various healing modalities: pressure, rubbing or kneading, tapping, and vibration. Pressure may be applied lightly to improve circulation and relieve sensations of chilling and numbness in the extremities. It is often combined with Oriental principles of pressure points and used for various types of pain control and anesthesia, which will be discussed later. Rubbing or kneading is used to relieve muscle spasms and improve circulation. This type of massage may also facilitate peristaltic action when applied to the abdomen. Tapping is done to mechanically loosen thick mucous obstructions in the lungs and bronchial tree of persons with asthma and cystic fibrosis. Vibration is used as a technique to shake a muscle to relieve sensations of numbness and facilitate the flow of energy that is trapped.

Keegan (1988b) notes that the Oriental tradition of acupressure is one of the oldest known methods of healing that is currently enjoying new appreciation in the Western world. Acupressure involves applying pressure with the finger or knuckle over pressure points located along meridians, which are the pathways by which energy flows through the body (Owens & Ehrenreich, 1991). The Japanese massage technique known as shiatsu literally means finger *(shi)* pressure *(atsu)* and involves prolonged pressure and spiritual concentration. While ordinary pressure massage tends to stimulate circulation and increase heartbeat, shiatsu activates the parasympathetic branch of the nervous system and produces relaxation (Kaslof, 1978).

Therapeutic Touch   Therapeutic Touch (TT) is a healing intervention based on the assumption that healer and healee are connected in a reciprocal relationship with interconnected energy fields. Essential to this relationship is the intention of the healer to focus positively on a healing outcome for the recipient of this intervention. The intervention was introduced into the nursing literature by Dolores Krieger in the 1970s as a healing meditation based on the ritual of the laying on of hands (Krieger, 1975).

Further development of this technique has been reported by Krieger (1987) who claims that a healing attitude of the nurse comes from focused inner awareness. This inner awareness requires that the healer focus on the intention or need to help another person. By first concentrating on being centered with all of one's energy directed in the present time (here and now) toward the intention of healing another, the nurse healer is then ready for intuitive and transcendent awareness. After achieving this awareness, the healer assesses the energy field of the healee by using the hands to search for a block in the healee's energy field. Krieger (1987) asserts that the impression received is merely an extension of the healer's sense of touch.

Several nurses have conducted research on the effects of TT as a healing modality in various populations (Gagne & Toye, 1994; Heidt, 1981). One delightful report is from Janet Quinn (1992) who taught the technique to elderly clients at a peer counseling center in California. Analysis of both quantitative data and qualitative responses from the participants provided evidence that learning TT resulted in healing among this population. Their responses to a question about what learning TT meant to them were statements such as being more aware of their bodies, feeling new possibilities, and feeling connected to others on a deeper level. One person responded that TT "makes me realize that one's whole person must be treated in order to have real healing" (p. 32).

THE ART OF HEALING

Healing is a process of recognizing a unity of life. It emphasizes the harmony between a person and the environment. Because a person experiences the environment through the senses, the environment is a very important factor to address in the art of healing. The art of healing, however, goes beyond ticking off the items on a checklist of healing ingredients. Art, by definition, is the expression of aesthetic qualities; it is the production and appreciation of what is beautiful, appealing, and pleasing (*Webster's Unabridged Dictionary of the English Language*, 1989). When the term is used in connection with healing, it requires an understanding that healing can occur without physiological changes associated with curing of diseases. Because healing involves the whole person relative to the environment, what is beautiful, appealing, and pleasing to that person must be considered of utmost importance for the purpose of healing.

In his book entitled *The Healer's Art*, Cassell (1976), a physician, identifies the difference between the mainstream focus of medicine on the cure of disease and the neglected art of healing. He asserts that the focus of medicine on disease and the application of technology is a narrow view of the larger issue of caring for people who are sick. He adds that this narrow view is but one of many ways to conceptualize and organize what nursing recognizes as the human health experience (Newman, Sime, & Corcoran-Perry, 1991). Society learns to expect certain outcomes from the stated focus of a discipline. American medicine focuses primarily on the treatment of disease. However, when people are in need of healing, much more than the scientific application of facts and technology is required. Several nurse theorists have stated their beliefs that the discipline of nursing is based on the primacy of caring and healing (Levine, 1973; Newman, 1986;

Watson, 1988). Caring and healing are aesthetic expressions of the natural harmony between human life and the universe at large.

Nursing theorist Myra Levine (1973) identified the nurse as the professional that promoted healing by reintegration of wholeness in a client. This nurse theorist understood that the healing process occurs over a period of time and because nurses are the people who spend the most time with patients or clients, they have a powerful influence on the healing process of those in their care. Levine, like Nightingale, emphasized the importance of paying attention to the environment and conserving the person's energy for healing. Newman (1986) identified health as expanding consciousness. This nurse theorist understood disease as one aspect of a person's pattern of health. Although she does not use the term *healing* directly, she presents the evolution of consciousness as the integration of opposites such as disease and nondisease. With this expanding consciousness, a person is able to exert more control in the choices she makes in response to the environment. This process points to the part that conscious awareness plays in healing.

As previously noted in chapter 2, Jean Watson (1988) provides a sound philosophy and set of propositions concerning the nature of nursing. She holds the position that caring is the essence and focus of nursing practice. Caring is expressed through interpersonal communication and is universal, crossing cultural boundaries. Aesthetic qualities of the caring process exemplified in nursing practice include the nurse's presence, touch, empathy, and giving time. Watson includes self-understanding or sensitivity to oneself as well as to others as essential to the interactive caring process.

Schroeder and Maeve (1992) applied Watson's theory of nursing as the art and science of transpersonal caring and healing to the care of persons living with HIV/AIDS. They discuss a model of nursing care partnerships that is highly individualized and empowering to nurses, clients, and supporting agencies. Using an analogy of a journey at sea, the nursing care partnership is seen as "a vessel that will help transport the client, with the help of the nursing care partner, through the often choppy waters of the health care system and the rough seas of HIV/AIDS" (p. 29). An example of aesthetic knowledge in this practice setting is the use of storytelling. According to Schroeder and Maeve, storytelling helps both nurses and clients to make meaning of their experiences through the journey of nursing care partnerships within the context of HIV/AIDS. It is a type of self-knowledge that enables the nurse and client to share intimate examples of their personal experiences without losing a protective distance between them.

As noted earlier, Johnson (1991) argues convincingly that nursing is both a science and an art. She reiterates that there is an essential relationship between these two qualities of the discipline of nursing and that "the nature of the art of nursing has primacy over the nature of the science of nursing" (p. 9). Johnson asserts that nursing science exists to serve the art of the discipline and not the other way around. Nursing art, according to Johnson, is useful and, by definition, refers to the practical know-how used by a nurse to achieve a particular result in an individualized situation. The purpose of nursing as an art, then, is for the nurse to do practical things objectively, such as caring well for another human being.

Price (1993) conducted a qualitative study of parents of children who were hospitalized to identify what quality of nursing care meant to these parents. She found that the parents described a process of getting to know the nurse as a key ingredient in quality of care. Technical skills were important also, but what the parents wanted most was time from the nurse in getting to know the child and family in a more personal way. This included listening to the parents and helping them to feel comfortable in the hospital environment, showing interest and concern for the child and parents, and individualizing the nursing care. The parents also thought quality of nursing care included the nurse showing affection and sensitivity to both child and parents. These are examples of the art of nursing expressed by nurses applying aesthetic knowledge in the healing process of providing care.

Bournaki and Germain (1993) add that aesthetics "enables the nurse to perceive the significance or meaning of a situation and to envision the results of the endpoint of her selected actions" (p. 83). Creative aspects of this aesthetic process include engaging, interpreting, and envisioning. This necessitates the nurse's understanding of the uniqueness of individuals in relation to their complexity, significance of context, values, and use of creativity. Aesthetics is the expressive dimension of nursing action. It is implicit in much nursing literature but needs to be made more explicit.

Returning to the vignette with which this chapter began, Beverly introduced aesthetics into the healing environment in which she met Mindy. By focusing on Mindy's perception of people and experiences throughout her childhood, Beverly practiced the art of nursing. Her use of visual stimuli to link outward behavior to inner feelings resulted in healing a schism that had divorced Mindy's concept of herself from her physical body and from her emotions.

Attending to the healing environment includes the notion of aesthetics: incorporating into caring relationships those things that are pleasing to the senses. Through the positive use of visual, auditory, olfactory, and gustatory stimuli, the environment can be enhanced for healing encounters. Moreover, the appropriate use of various forms of touch, including massage or the transfer of energy, can also be used to facilitate healing.

References

Bournaki, M., & Germain, C. P. (1993). Esthetic knowledge in family-centered nursing care of hospitalized children. *Advances in Nursing Science, 16* (2), 81–89.

Carper, B. A. (1978). Fundamental patterns of knowing in nursing. *Advances in Nursing Science, 1* (1), 13–23.

Cassell, E. J. (1976). *The healer's art.* Philadelphia: J. B. Lippincott Company.

Cooper, D. M. (1990). Optimizing wound healing: A practice within nursing's domain. *Nursing Clinics of North America, 25* (1), 165–180.

Dieckmann, H. (1973). Theories of beauty to the mid-nineteenth century. In P. P. Wiener (Ed.), *Dictionary of the history of ideas* (Vol. 1) (pp. 195–206). New York: Charles Scribner's Sons.

Ferguson, E. D. (1901). The evolution of the trained nurse. *American Journal of Nursing, 1* (9), 625.

Gagne, D., & Toye, R. C. (1994). The effects of Therapeutic Touch and relaxation therapy in reducing anxiety. *Archives of Psychiatric Nursing, 8,* 184–189.

Heidt, P. (1981). Effect of Therapeutic Touch on anxiety levels of hospitalized patients. *Nursing Research, 30,* 32–37.

Johnson, J. (1991). Nursing science: Basic, applied, or practical? Implications for the art of nursing. *Advances in Nursing Science, 14* (1), 7–16.

Kaslof, L. J. (1978). *Wholistic dimensions in healing.* Garden City, NY: Doubleday & Company, Inc.

Keegan, L. (1988a). Environment: Protecting our personal and planetary home. In B. M. Dossey, L. Keegan, C. E. Guzzetta, & L. G. Kolkmeier, *Holistic nursing: A handbook for practice* (pp. 181–194). Rockville, MD: Aspen Publishers, Inc.

Keegan, L. (1988b). Touch: Connecting with the healing power. In B. M. Dossey, L. Keegan, C. E. Guzzetta, & L. G. Kolkmeier, *Holistic nursing: A handbook for practice* (pp. 331–355). Rockville, MD: Aspen Publishers, Inc.

Krieger, D. (1975). Therapeutic Touch: The imprimatur of nursing. *American Journal of Nursing, 75* (5), 784–787.

Krieger, D. (1987). *Living the therapeutic touch.* New York: Dodd, Mead & Co.

Levine, M. (1973). *Introduction to clinical nursing* (2nd ed.). Philadelphia: F. A. Davis.

Newman, M. A. (1986). *Health as expanding consciousness.* St. Louis: C. V. Mosby Company.

Newman, M. A., Sime, A. M., & Corcoran-Perry, S. A. (1991). The focus of the discipline of nursing. *Advances in Nursing Science, 14* (1), 1–6.

Nightingale, F. (1946). *Notes on nursing: What it is, and what it is not.* Philadelphia: J. B. Lippincott Company (Facsimile of the first edition, printed in London, 1859)

Owens, M. K., & Ehrenreich, D. (1991). Application of nonpharmacologic methods of managing chronic pain. *Holistic Nursing Practice, 6* (1), 32–40.

Perlaky, D. (1994). A bearable solution. *Nursing 94, 24* (1), 60–62.

Poppel, E. (1988). *Mindworks: Time and conscious experience.* Boston: Harcourt Brace Jovanovich, Publishers.

Price, P. J. (1993). Parents' perceptions of the meaning of quality nursing care. *Advances in Nursing Science, 16* (1), 33–41.

Quinn, J. F. (1992). The senior's Therapeutic Touch education program. *Holistic Nursing Practice, 7* (1), 32–37.

Rossi, E. L., & Cheek, D. B. (1988). *Mind-body therapy: Ideodynamic healing in hypnosis.* New York: W. W. Norton & Company.

Schorr, J. A. (1993). Music and pattern change in chronic pain. *Advances in Nursing Science, 15* (4), 27–36.

Schroeder, C., & Maeve, M. K. (1992). Nursing care partnerships at the Denver Nursing Project in Human Caring: An application and extension of caring theory in practice. *Advances in Nursing Science, 15* (2), 25–38.

Shipley, J. T. (1945). *Dictionary of word origins.* New York: Dorset Press.

Simonton, O. C., & Henson, R. (1992). *The healing journey.* New York: Bantam Books.

Simonton, O. C., Matthews-Simonton, S., & Creighton, J. (1978). *Getting well again.* Los Angeles: J. P. Tarcher.

Sobel, D. S. (1990). The placebo effect: Using the body's own healing mechanisms. In R. Ornstein & C. Swencionis (Eds.), *The healing brain: A scientific reader* (pp. 63–74). New York: The Guilford Press.

Taylor, R. (1994). Brave new nose: Sniffing out human sexual chemistry. *The Journal of NIH Research, 6* (1), 47–51.

Watson, J. (1988). *Nursing: Human science and human care.* New York: National League for Nursing.

Webster's unabridged dictionary of the English language. (1989). New York: Portland House.

Whipple, B., & Glynn, N. J. (1992). Quantification of the effects of listening to music as a noninvasive method of pain control. *Scholarly Inquiry for Nursing Practice: An International Journal, 6* (1), 43–58.

Wood, B. M. (1926). The psychology of trays. *American Journal of Nursing, 26* (12), 947–949.

Wurtman, R. J. (1990). Ways that foods can affect the brain. In R. Ornstein & C. Swencionis (Eds.), *The healing brain: A scientific reader.* New York: The Guilford Press.

Zahourek, R. P. (Ed.). (1988). *Relaxation & imagery: Tools for therapeutic communication and intervention.* Philadelphia: W. B. Saunders Company.

Zeki, S. (1993). *A vision of the brain.* Oxford: Blackwell Scientific Publications.

Suggested Reading

Birx, E. (1991). *Content analysis of peak experiences in nursing practice.* Unpublished doctoral dissertation, School of Nursing, The University of Texas at Austin.

Brennan, B. A. (1988). *Hands of light.* New York: Bantam Books.

Lynch, J. J. (1990). The broken heart: The psychobiology of human contact. In R. Ornstein & C. Swencionis (Eds.), *The healing brain: A scientific reader* (pp. 75–87). New York: The Guilford Press.

Quinn, J. F., & Streklauskas, A. J. (1993). Psychoimmunologic effects of Therapeutic Touch on practitioners and recently bereaved recipients: A pilot study. *Advances in Nursing Science, 15* (4), 13–26.

5 | PERSONAL KNOWLEDGE AND INTUITION

When I sit still and listen to my body, it tells me things that I can't open to in other ways. There is a constant hum that can be heard and it's my own vibration. This can only be sensed in silence. It's soothing and healing.

L. Berman, 1992

Jane

Jane was 46 years old when she fell at the grocery store and injured her ankle. Spraining her ankle was not an uncommon event for Jane. She had sustained similar injuries many times before in her life and she knew it would take rest and patience to recover once again, allowing her body to heal itself. What was unique and frightening about this particular injury was that less than 6 months ago she had broken the same ankle and the sudden realization that she was once again in pain and would have a period of convalescence to face was more than she could bear at that moment.

When Jane was examined by the orthopedic surgeon who had treated her for the broken ankle a few months earlier, he asked her how painful this new injury was compared with the break. Jane looked at him blankly and then replied, "I don't know; give me a few minutes to get back into the pain." She then shifted awareness to the pain in her ankle and began to sob, saying, "I think it hurts worse and I just can't take any more pain right now. Please excuse me, but I have to hypnotize myself again so the pain will retreat."

Jane's story is but one example of the kind of personal knowledge that facilitates healing. In a deeply personal way, Jane instantly and intuitively knew that her body was injured and that she had so many other demands on her person at that time that she simply could not allow herself to give in to sensations of pain and let them control her. Intellectually she knew that the pain was a signal that there was injury or malfunction in a part of the body and, consequently, warranted her attention. She also knew from various personal experiences that focusing her attention on the pain would make it more intense whereas focusing on a different picture where the pain is only part of a larger reality would make it more manageable.

PERSONAL KNOWLEDGE

Personal knowledge refers to a person's individualized and subjective ways of learning, storing, and retrieving information about the world. From the moment of birth, a person shares experiences with others in the world yet this experience has a personal meaning that cannot be fully appreciated by any other human being. Objective knowledge of things and events represents information shared as reality among people while subjective knowledge is individually interpreted and perceived as real.

Personal knowledge is more than knowledge about oneself. Carper (1978) asserts that personal knowledge is concerned with knowing, encountering, and actualizing one's individual self in relation to other human beings. In a helping and healing relationship between two people, both individuals risk knowing and being known authentically by the other person. This involves risk and vulnerability so that sharing and connecting can occur. It denies any type of hierarchical order where one individual has power over another. It emphasizes the dynamic process of each individual. Neither is considered a static object.

In a delightful and provocative article about the patterns of knowing that Carper identified in nursing, Peggy Chinn (1989) recounts her dream of a place she calls a Healing House. In the dream she describes a setting that was simple yet comfortable and homelike. People at the Healing House helped her to relax and suggested that she listen to music to maintain her sense of peace. They told her that she might not leave the house cured of the disease that had brought her there, but that she would leave knowing that she had within her a healing spirit that would help her to have a healthier life. The Healing House of her dream was in sharp contrast to the reality of the gloomy hospital room where she suddenly awoke from the dream. Chinn goes on to address patterns of knowing, including personal knowledge, that are needed if persons are to be healed and to assist in the healing of others. She states that such knowing must move away from valuing only the traditional objective facts of empirical science and move toward the integration of all aspects of one's experience. Such personal knowing also moves away from issues of dominating and controlling people toward creating choices for each other and empowering one another. She emphasizes that these choices and this type of empowerment are very personal. Finally, Chinn asserts that dreams such as hers of the Healing House can come true by beginning to act with conscious awareness and taking steps toward making reality out of dreamed ideals.

Michael Polanyi (1962), a chemist and philosopher, writes about personal knowledge in a book whose purpose is to argue against the notion of scientific objectivity. He asserts that objective knowing requires "*personal participation* of the knower in all acts of understanding" (p. vii, italics in the original). He adds that comprehension is a responsible act and an intellectual commit ment. For Polanyi, "facts about living things are more highly personal than the facts of the inanimate world" (p. 347). Science, based on a philosophy of empiricism and objectivity, does produce facts about the inanimate world. But as Polanyi argues, what we know about living and healing cannot possibly be objective in the same sense as what we know about objects. Because healing is a process, personal knowledge that is dynamic and subjective is essential to this process. Similarly, because healing often takes place through relationships, personal knowledge is of prime importance.

In recent years, an increasing amount of research in nursing has utilized qualitative methodologies. Such methods as grounded theory and phenomenology emphasize the importance of understanding social processes and lived experiences of people rather than predicting outcomes based on conceptual or mathematical models. Although rigor is as essential to the process of conducting qualitative research as it is to conducting quantitative studies, acknowledgment of the investigator's personal involvement and personal knowledge is a distinct difference found only in the former. Linda Dunn (1991) describes the personal awareness that she developed while conducting a phenomenological study of women who had been battered. She noted that during the time when she was collecting and analyzing data, she experienced many physical and emotional problems but was not immediately aware that these had any connection to her professional work. She stated that she had difficulty sleeping, poor digestion, severe headaches, and shoulder and neck pain. These disorders paralleled the responses of the women she was studying! Needless to say, gaining awareness of this personal response was essential for the researcher to understand and interpret the experiences of the informants in her study correctly. Through a process of self-reflection and social support, she developed personal knowledge that enabled her to respond in a more healthy manner to the stress of conducting this type of study.

Marlaine Smith (1992), a nurse researcher at the University of Colorado, argues that personal knowing is primary to all other ways of knowing. She states that the way we come to know the world is based on our personal beliefs and preferences. The meaning we attach to objects and events is similarly connected to that which we value. The decisions we make about our actions are also based on our personal worldviews and values. Awareness and acknowledgment of our personal biases and values, then, influence the way in which we see all of the experiences of our living. Personal knowledge affects the relationship each person has with the universe. To view the world as threatening and hostile is to experience disharmony and illness, whereas to view the world as supporting and friendly is to experience harmony and health.

Claire B. Draucker (1992), a nursing faculty member at Kent State University, conducted a grounded theory study of 11 women who were survivors of incest. What she discovered in interviewing these women was that they experienced healing as a process similar to constructing a residence. These women described tasks of healing that involved hard work such as digging away, struggling against challenges within the environment, and designing and creating a new way to live in the world. Draucker points out that the healing process for these women included three primary elements: "building a new relationship with the self to provide nurturing and security; regulating one's relationships with others; and influencing the community in a meaningful way" (p. 6). The first component of building a new relationship with the self may be viewed as an example of personal knowledge in which old beliefs and understandings about personal responsibility for the incest are replaced by new insights and new responsibilities for self-care. Healing of the deepest incest wounds may depend on this basis of personal knowledge.

A relatively new concept identified by Budd (1993) as self-coherence provides another way to view personal knowledge and its relationship to the human health experience. Self-coherence is defined as "the ability to integrate present experience with past experience, motivations and goals, and to find meaning in the present experience" (p. 366). Self-coherence consists of three central ideas. The first is the person's awareness of transactions with the environment. These transactions include the input of information and the exchange of matter and energy. The second idea comprising self-coherence is the integration of environmental transactions with the person's motivations and goals. This idea is traced to psychological conceptualizations of the self as both a process and product. In the course of human development, each person constructs a personal scheme of reality which usually lies outside the person's usual awareness. When a person successfully integrates transactions with the environment, that person is aware of the self and knows what the self needs to maintain health and well-being. The third idea contained in the concept of self-coherence is a connectedness to the person's source of inner strength. Budd again refers to other psychological theories of personality development and indicates that people who find meaning in life and enjoy high levels of health and well-being have achieved a deep self-knowledge about their connectedness with other persons and the world at large.

Personal knowledge is unique to each individual and, therefore, it is essential to each person's subjective relationship with the universe. Each person selects information to be attended to and to be stored in memory. Bits of information are sorted and classified in unique systems within each person. Meaning is added to the person's experiences with each object and event encountered. This meaning cannot be exactly the same as the meaning ascribed to the same object or event encountered by another person. Perceptions of real events and objects are individualized. Experiences of health and illness are also unique to each individual and may be understood best through direct knowing or intuition.

INTUITION

Intuition is a human experience of sudden or immediate knowledge that has been the subject of both mystical fascination and scientific skepticism. It has been addressed by philosophers, mathematicians, educators, psychologists, theologians, business managers, and health professionals. It has a long history of being valued by many Eastern cultures and only recently has been greeted with new respect in this country. Early Greek philosophers such as Plato and Aristotle considered intuition as a valid and reliable form of truth or of reality (Noddings & Shore, 1984). As a human cognitive skill, intuition is central to our understanding of the personal knowledge that is needed in the process of healing.

Intuition and Experts from History

Three world-famous experts well-known among scientific disciplines who trusted their intuitions are Archimedes, Kekulé, and Einstein. Archimedes was a Greek mathematician who lived from

287 to 212 B.C. He spent most of his life in Sicily and was responsible for defining the principle of the lever. He invented the hydraulic screw or spiral pump, known as Archimedes' screw, which is still used in Egypt and other countries for raising water from a lower level to a higher one. The Law of Hydrostatics is the discovery that links the name of Archimedes with the concept of intuition.

The story of Archimedes' famous discovery goes something like this: During the Roman conquest of Sicily, King Hieron consulted Archimedes often to develop various methods of defeating the Romans. He also asked Archimedes to determine whether his crown, which was supposed to be made of pure gold, also contained some silver or other less precious metal. Archimedes analyzed this problem for several days and seemed to be getting nowhere near a solution that would satisfy the suspicious king. One day as Archimedes stepped into his bathtub and observed the overflow of water, the solution to the mystery came to him in an instant. He just knew that the weight of the crown could be determined by the amount of water displaced and that the solution to the mystery could come from measuring equal amounts of gold and silver and the amounts of water each of them displaced. He was so relieved and excited about this flash of knowledge that he ran home without his clothes, running through the streets shouting "Eureka! Eureka!," which means "I have found it."

From this intuitive grasp of the situation, Archimedes established what is sometimes referred to as Archimedes' principle, which states that a body immersed in fluid displaces liquid of an equal weight. And the term *Eureka* has come to be identified with a sudden insight or awareness of certain knowledge.

Hundreds of years later, the German chemist, Kekulé, had a similar experience. Friedrich August von Kekulé had been struggling with carbon compounds and had made brilliant strides in identifying the trivalent structure of many organic substances. But he was stumped by the specific structure of benzene, which had been discovered in 1825 by the English scientist Michael Faraday. One evening in 1865, Kekulé was relaxing by his fireplace and became mesmerized by watching the flames. In his words,

*. . . the atoms were gambolling before my eyes. This time the
smaller groups kept modestly in the background. My mental eye,
rendered more acute by repeated visions of this kind, could now
distinguish larger structures, of manifold conformation; long
rows, sometimes more closely fitted together; all twining and twist-
ing in snakelike motion. But look! What was that? One of the
snakes had seized hold of its own tail and the form whirled mock-
ingly before my eyes. As if by a flash of lightning, I awoke. . .*

(Goldberg, 1983, p. 76)

Suddenly, Kekulé knew that a ring, not an open structure, was
the solution to the representation of benzene. This discovery was
instrumental as a basic theory for the development of the entire
field of organic chemistry. Again, intuition was the cognitive skill
that brought the truth into Kekulé's awareness.

Similarly, Albert Einstein, the German American theoretical
physicist of more recent times, had this to say about the discovery of natural laws: "There are no logical paths to these laws,
only intuition resting on sympathetic understanding of experience
can reach them" (Goldberg, 1983, p. 21). The essence of many
scientific breakthroughs is that they defy our usual assumptions
and go beyond what we have any logical reason to expect.
Einstein's theory of general relativity itself is an example. Einstein
states that he had what he referred to as "the happiest thought
of my life"; he realized that a person falling from a roof was both
at rest and in motion at the same time (Goldberg, 1983, p. 22) —
a very illogical thought. However, years later when the theory
gained proof, Einstein again acknowledged the importance of
intuition as an essential ingredient in discovery.

Women's Intuition

Intuition has often been referred to as "women's intuition" and
there are plenty of examples of important happenings related to
the intuitive insight of women. In the countries of Russia, Poland,
Romania, Yugoslavia, and others along the Baltic Sea, a story is
told of a little girl named Vasalisa that depicts intuition as the trea-
sure of a woman's psyche. The story begins with a paradox,
"Once there was, and once there was not." According to Estés

(1992), who relates the story in more detail, this paradox reminds us of the fairy-tale quality of the story. The gist of the story is as follows.

Vasalisa

There once was, and was not, a young mother who lay dying while her daughter and husband sat at the end of her bed. The daughter, Vasalisa, was called by her mother to receive a blessing from her deathbed. Mustering what little strength she had left, the mother presented her daughter with a tiny doll dressed just like Vasalisa in a black skirt, white apron, a vest embroidered with brightly colored threads, and bright red boots. As she presented Vasalisa with the little doll, the mother said, "Here are my last words, Beloved. Should you lose your way or be in need of help, ask this doll what to do. You will be assisted. Keep the doll with you always. Do not tell anyone about her. Feed her when she is hungry. This is my mother's promise to you, my blessing on you, dear daughter" (Estés, 1992, pp. 75–76). And with that brief but profound message, Vasalisa's mother drew her last breath and died.

After a period of mourning, Vasalisa's father remarried and much like Cinderella, Vasalisa found herself waiting hand and foot on a new stepmother and her two daughters who were not as sweet and beautiful as the blessed Vasalisa. So the stepmother and her two daughters conspired to harm Vasalisa. They arranged for the fire to go out in their house and when she came inside for the evening, the stepmother told Vasalisa that she would have to go into the woods to retrieve the fire so the family would be warm and able to cook again. Vasalisa's task was to find the old witch, Baba Yaga, who they were sure would kill and eat Vasalisa. In her innocent obedience, Vasalisa did as she was directed by the wicked stepmother and went out into the woods in search of Baba Yaga.

Vasalisa set out to find Baba Yaga, but the night became darker and she was unfamiliar with the way. As she started to feel frightened, she reached into the pocket of her apron and found the doll that her dying mother had blessed her with. She patted the doll and realized this did make her feel better. Whenever she came to a fork in the path and was uncertain which way to go, she consulted the doll who directed her to go this way or that. At last, Vasalisa came to the hut where Baba Yaga lived and she found that the old witch was a very scary creature with greasy hair, a chin that curved up, and a nose that curved down, and she had warts that looked as if they belonged on a toad. Her house was equally scary as it sat upon huge yellow scaly chicken legs and the bolts on the doors and shutters were made of human toes and fingers.

Vasalisa was reassured by the little doll in the red boots that this was the right house and so she said to Baba Yaga, "I have come for fire because my family is cold and cannot cook without it." Baba Yaga quickly retorted that she knew the family's fire had gone out and asked Vasalisa why she thought she should give it to her. Vasalisa was at a loss for a response, but consulted the doll in her pocket and quickly said, "Because I ask" (Estés, 1992, p. 78). Baba Yaga was surprised and replied, "You are lucky, that is the correct answer, but before I can give you any fire, you must perform the tasks I give you to do." Again, Vasalisa complied and listened while Baba Yaga outlined a long, long list of laundry and cooking and cleaning tasks. Then Baba Yaga flew off into the night with a warning that Vasalisa would be her feast if the tasks were not done when she returned. Feeling overwhelmed by the responsibility of returning fire to her family's home and of completing the witch's work in a timely manner, Vasalisa again consulted her tiny doll and asked if it would be possible for her to do all that she had been commanded to complete. The small doll reassured her and encouraged her also to get some sleep. In the morning, Vasalisa discovered that the doll had done all the work.

When Baba Yaga returned, she sneered at Vasalisa, ate her enormous supper and then said to Vasalisa, "You must do the same tasks again tomorrow." And pointing to a mound of dirt in the yard, she added, "In that pile of dirt are many poppy seeds and I want in the morning to see one pile of dirt and one pile of poppy seeds." When Baba Yaga left, Vasalisa again consulted the doll and asked how she would ever get that job done, and once again the tiny doll reassured her and in the morning when Baba Yaga returned, the tasks were completed. The witch again reminded Vasalisa that she was a lucky girl and Vasalisa began to ask Baba Yaga questions until the little doll in her pocket began to jump violently warning Vasalisa to stop asking so many questions. At long last, Baba Yaga told Vasalisa to be on her way and to take with her a skull with fiery eyes on a stick. Vasalisa ran home while the little doll told her which way to turn. When the stepmother and the sisters saw Vasalisa running toward their home with the fiery skull, they were shocked because they were sure her long absence meant that she was dead by now. But Vasalisa brought the skull with the fiery eyes into the home and the eyes watched all that the stepmother and sisters did and by morning the skull with the fiery eyes had burned them into cinders.

This story, told by Clarissa Estés (1992) in her book, *Women Who Run with the Wolves,* is about the power and blessing of women's intuition. The power and gift of intuition is characterized in the story by the multiple dimensions of inner knowing, inner hearing, and inner seeing that are represented by Vasalisa's little doll with the red boots. It is a wonderful reminder that the capacity for wisdom is inherent within human beings.

There are also many current examples of women's intuition from the field of business. These include Debbie Fields, president and CEO of Mrs. Fields Cookies. Drawing on her emotional need to bake cookies and offer them to her friends to help them feel happy as teenagers, she fought the logical reasons for not starting a cookie company and now enjoys a multimillion-dollar success story with over 200 stores in the United States, Asia, and Australia. Similarly, Mary Kay Ash decided to retire in 1963 after a ho-hum career in catalog sales. Upon retirement she thought about writing a book to help women overcome the obstacles they experienced in business careers. But Mary Kay didn't know how to write a book. So she started jotting down notes to herself about all the things she thought were barriers to women's career advancement. The notes turned out not to be a prospectus for a book, but the marketing plan for Mary Kay Cosmetics (Rowan, 1986).

Recent empirical research lends some support to the notion of women's intuition as a special phenomenon related to hormonal differences between men and women. The hormone oxytocin released during menstruation and pregnancy may be responsible for placing women in a more receptive frame of mind. This, coupled with evidence that the structure of the corpus callosum, a bundle of fibers connecting the two hemispheres of the brain, is thicker in women than in men suggests that differences in intuitive perception may have some basis in biological differences based on gender. Social conditioning that permits intuitive thinking in girls and squelches it in boys may be another factor that contributes to differences found between the sexes in their preferences for intuitive thinking and judgment (Yudkin, 1993).

Intuition Defined

These examples of famous men and their scientific discoveries and famous women and their enormously successful businesses reflect an important common element in the development of expertise: trust in and reliance on their intuitive grasp of complicated situations. In particular, the common elements are that the intuitive grasp of the expert is needed when problems are extremely complex, conditions are uncertain, and the solution comes instantly as a perceived whole.

Just what is intuition? Intuition has been referred to as the "third eye" as well as the "sixth sense." It has much of its historical roots in two very different disciplines: the mathematical axiom, which is a self-evident proposition that requires no proof, and the religious or mystical idea of revelation — the idea or belief that revealed knowledge or truth surpasses the analytic powers of the human intellect. Furthermore, numerous ancient mathematicians such as Pythagoras and Greek philosophers provide much of the historical basis for our understanding of this complex and fascinating phenomenon today.

Spinoza, a Greek philosopher, asserted that intuition is the highest form of intelligence and surpasses empirical knowledge gained only from sensory experiences and scientific knowledge gained from reasoning. Immanuel Kant, another philosopher, identified intuition as a component of perception that was supplied by the mind itself. For example, Kant believed that human beings could apprehend space and time only as pure intuitions. Space and time, according to Kant, cannot be understood through the linear, analytic process of reasoning. Bergson differentiated analytic from synthetic thinking. Intuition, according to Bergson, is a type of instinct that allows us to deal with the fundamental nature of life and thought. He proposed that analysis produces what is relative about an object while intuition produces that which is individual or absolute. Each of these philosophers asserted that intuition is different from the linear reasoning process of analysis.

Until recently, the concept of intuition has not been taken seriously or valued in scientific disciplines, especially in this country. However, in the past decade, a number of researchers in diverse fields such as mathematics, education, business administration, and my own discipline of nursing have systematically studied this aspect of human intelligence. Intuition is defined in several different ways by each discipline, but at least three attributes are inherent in all:

1. Knowledge is immediate

2. Knowledge is received as a whole

3. Knowledge occurs in the absence of a conscious analytic process of reasoning. (Rew, 1986)

In recent years, there has been an increased interest in the phenomenon of intuition as an important component in skilled clinical judgment in nursing. Several nurse researchers have conducted descriptive studies in which the concept of intuition is clearly identified by practicing nurses as a skill that comes with years of experience (Agan, 1987; Benner & Tanner, 1987; Rew, 1988, 1990, 1991; Schraeder & Fisher, 1986, 1987).

Intuition is a way of knowing something without knowing how or why one knows it. It is a universal skill that is frequently seen in children but is rarely acknowledged and nourished in the American culture. Consequently, we do not know how to use its full potential in the process of healing. The Italian psychotherapist and originator of the theory of psychosynthesis, Roberto Assagioli (1976), refers to intuition as a valid means of knowing and traces the meaning of the word to its origin in the Latin: *in tueri*, which means to see within. With this type of meaning, intuition is obviously important to our discussion of awareness in healing.

Intuition can take place under many different circumstances and is usually accompanied by physical sensations that are associated with arousal of the autonomic nervous system. Each individual has his own unique system that is alerted when an intuition occurs. Each of you might be thinking of a situation in which you "just knew" something was true, but you couldn't give a reason why it should be so. If you reflect on such an experience, you might also be aware of a physical sensation that accompanied the immediate apprehension of the phenomenon such as a chill going up your spine or getting goose bumps on your arms. Other people feel a knot or butterflies in their stomachs; hence, the origin of the term *gut feeling* to signal the arrival of an intuitive truth.

David Loye, in his book entitled *The Sphinx and the Rainbow* (1983), classified three types of intuition. The first is precognition, the second is cognitive inference, and the third is gestalt. Precognition is the least understood of the types of intuition. It concerns knowledge that predicts future events. Many people have had this type of experience where there is a sense of anticipation or impending doom that a particular event will take place. Nurses have described many such experiences. For example, one nurse was admitting a patient to the critical care unit. He was experiencing chest pains, but all the signs and symptoms indicated a stomach problem, for which medical treatment had been ordered. The nurse, on the other hand, had a strong feeling that he was going to die of a heart attack. Within 3 hours, he experienced a sudden cardiac arrest and died. The autopsy confirmed her prediction.

The second type of intuition is the one that all of us experience as we become more familiar with a particular subject.

Cognitive inference involves the rapid processing of sensory cues that have become like second nature to us. Whereas we initially learn to solve problems in a linear fashion, taking one logical step at a time, through practice we develop performance skills or expertise that allow us to put these cues together to form a whole without even consciously thinking about the process. Looking back to your own experiences with arithmetic and mathematics as an example, remember the first time you learned to add 2 and 2. You probably counted on your fingers, or counted the total number of apples in a visual representation of the problem. Very quickly you learned the answer to the problem through memorization ($2 + 2 = 4$). This basic knowledge becomes so easy after awhile that the anlaytic process is no longer consciously thought about when solving more complex variations of the problem such as 2 apples + 2 oranges = ? Through cognitive inference you conclude that the answer or solution is 4 pieces of fruit or some similar response. So mathematics offers us some of our first experiences with making cognitive inferences to know a solution to a problem as a whole, immediately, and without going through a linear problem-solving process.

The third type of intuition is called gestalt after the Gestalt school of psychology. *Gestalt* means form in German and this term was used by both German philosophers and psychologists to stress the importance of studying and perceiving entire patterns rather than individual elements in a particular form. Many experiments on perception and learning have shown how forms can be perceived as wholes without analysis of individual parts. A common example is the triangle that is perceived from three straight lines or from three dots (figure 5.1).

FIGURE 5.1   *Perceiving the whole*

Gestalt intuition stresses the synthesizing function of intuition as it closes gaps, as in the triangle composed of dots, and smoothes jagged edges to form a pattern of the whole picture. Another feature of gestalt intuition is the synthesis of facts or information in illogical combinations, such as the example of Einstein's musing that if he fell off a roof he would be both moving and at rest. In this form, intuition most closely resembles the related phenomenon of creativity, which will be addressed more fully in chapter 7.

As stated earlier, our Western culture has fallen in love with the results of an empirical philosophy and technology that value the linear reasoning process and downplay the value of intuition. Other barriers to developing our intuitive skills include our lack of understanding about how these processes work, our fear of taking risks in situations that are ambiguous and uncertain, and our lack of confidence in those phenomena that cannot be experienced through the five basic senses of sight, sound, smell, taste, or touch. Other factors that impede our use of intuition include anxiety, fatigue and emotional tension, rushing to make a decision, and acting impulsively (Agor, 1989).

There are several things people can do to begin to value and develop their intuitive skills. The first of these is to become well-acquainted with one's own method of solving a complex problem or making a difficult decision. Jot down all the words and feelings you associate with the word *intuition.* Talk to others about these associations. Be open to your imagination and practice imagining unusual things such as the space between your eyes or that you are wearing a space suit and experiencing weightlessness (Vaughan, 1979). All of these simple exercises serve to stimulate awareness of intuitive possibilities and many of these will be expanded upon in chapter 8 as methods to enhance awareness.

To facilitate an intuitive solution for a particular decision or problem, one must first learn to quiet the chatter of the busy, analytic mind. Several methods of relaxation will work: meditation, self-hypnosis, classical music, and progressive relaxation. Once relaxed and quieted, the mind can be directed to listen or look for an answer or solution that just comes effortlessly without searching directly for such an outcome.

PERSONAL KNOWLEDGE AND INTUITION IN HEALING

As suggested by Smith (1992), personal knowledge, or how we come to be aware of and make sense of the world, is basic to all other ways of knowing. To engage in healing ourselves or to be involved in healing through relationship with another begins with self-awareness. Dienstfrey (1992) refers to this as using the *aware mind*, which is the mind that operates in the light of consciousness. This awareness of how we view our unique situation and what we believe and expect will happen in these situations is the basis of our perception of what constitutes reality (Krieger, 1987). Such perception influences all the choices we make about how to act. Consequently, as self-awareness increases, the mind and the body are better able to work together for healing.

Intuition is evidence of a healing consciousness at work in the universe. The function of intuition brings seemingly disparate chunks of information together to form a whole or an insightful solution that was not forthcoming with the usual linear process of reasoning. Jane's story reflects the power of personal knowledge and intuition working in tandem to propel her into the process of healing. Intuition that is respected and honed into a source of inner knowing and strength becomes the best friend of both healer and healed. Awareness of this cognitive skill enables the nurse to act with a sense of calmness and certainty in a set of complex circumstances characterized by uncertainty and ambiguity. The nurse who is aware of expert knowledge refined over myriad experiences with subtle similarities and differences can respond in a variety of creative ways, as will be shown in chapter 7, to the person seeking a healing environment. A nurse who values her own intuition will also trust the client who shares personal intuitive insights about illness and health within the nurse-client relationship.

References

Agan, R. D. (1987). Intuitive knowing as a dimension of nursing. *Advances in Nursing Science, 10* (1), 63–70.

Agor, W. H. (Ed.). (1989). *Intuition in organizations.* Newbury Park, CA: Sage Publications, Inc.

Assagioli, R. (1976). *The act of will.* New York: Penguin.

Benner, P., & Tanner, C. (1987). Clinical judgment: How expert nurses use intuition. *American Journal of Nursing, 87,* 23–31.

Berman, L. (1992). Noetic perspectives on healing. *Institute of Noetic Sciences Bulletin, 7* (4), 10.

Budd, K. W. (1993). Self-coherence: Theoretical considerations of a new concept. *Archives of Psychiatric Nursing, 7,* 361–368.

Carper, B. A. (1978). Fundamental patterns of knowing in nursing. *Advances in Nursing Science, 1* (1), 13–23.

Chinn, P. L. (1989). Nursing patterns of knowing and feminist thought. *Nursing & Health Care, 19,* 71–75.

Dienstfrey, H. (1992). The aware mind. *Noetic Sciences Review, 21,* 17–20.

Draucker, C. B. (1992). The healing process of female adult incest survivors: Constructing a personal residence. *IMAGE: Journal of Nursing Scholarship, 24,* 4–8.

Dunn, L. (1991). Research alert! Qualitative research may be hazardous to your health! *Qualitative Health Research, 1,* 388–392.

Estés, C. P. (1992). *Women who run with the wolves.* New York: Ballantine.

Goldberg, P. (1983). *The intuitive edge.* Los Angeles: Jeremy P. Tarcher, Inc.

Krieger, D. (1987). *Living the therapeutic touch.* New York: Dodd, Mead & Co.

Loye, D. (1983). *The sphinx and the rainbow.* Boulder, CO: Shambhala Publications, Inc.

Noddings, N., & Shore, P. J. (1984). *Awakening the inner eye: Intuition in education.* New York: Teachers College Press.

Polanyi, M. (1962). *Personal knowledge.* Chicago: The University of Chicago Press.

Rew, L. (1986). Intuition: Concept analysis of a group phenomenon. *Advances in Nursing Science, 8* (2), 21–28.

Rew, L. (1988). Intuition in decision-making. *IMAGE: The Journal of Nursing Scholarship, 20,* 150–154.

Rew, L. (1990). Intuition in critical care nursing practice. *Dimensions of Critical Care Nursing, 9* (1), 30–37.

Rew, L. (1991). Intuition in psychiatric-mental health nursing. *Journal of Child and Adolescent Psychiatric and Mental Health Nursing, 4,* 110–115.

Rew, L., & Barrow, E. M. (1989). Nurses' intuition: Can it coexist with the nursing process? *Association of Operating Room Nurses Journal, 50,* 353–358.

Rowan, R. (1986). *The intuitive manager.* Boston: Little, Brown, and Co.

Schraeder, B. D., & Fischer, D. K. (1986). Using intuitive knowledge to make clinical decisions. *Maternal Child Nursing, 11,* 161–162.

Schraeder, B. D., & Fischer, D. K. (1987). Using intuitive knowledge in the neonatal intensive care nursery. *Holistic Nursing Practice, 1,* 45–51.

Smith, M. C. (1992). Is all knowing personal knowing? *Nursing Science Quarterly, 5* (1), 2–3.

Vaughan, F. E. (1979). *Awakening intuition.* New York: Doubleday.

Yudkin, M. (1993). Women's intuition: Is it just an old wives' tale? *Intuition, 1* (3), 20–23.

Suggested Reading

Agor, W. H. (1986). *The logic of intuitive decision making.* New York: Quorum Books.

Algase, D. L., & Whall, A. F. (1993). Rosemary Ellis' views on the substantive structure of nursing. *IMAGE: Journal of Nursing Scholarship, 25,* 69–72.

Bass, E., & Davis, L. (1988). *The courage to heal.* New York: Harper & Row.

Bastick, T. (1982). *Intuition: How we think and act.* New York: John Wiley & Sons.

Rew, L., Agor, W. H., Emery, M. R., & Harper, S. C. (1991). Intuitive skills in crisis management. *NursingConnections, 4* (2), 3–12.

Rew, L., & Barrow, E. M. (1987). Intuition: A neglected hallmark of nursing knowledge. *Advances in Nursing Science, 10* (1), 49–62.

Riegel, B., Omery, A., Calvillo, E., Elsayed, N. G., Lee, P., Shuler, P., & Siegal, B. E. (1992). Moving beyond: A generative philosophy of science. *IMAGE: Journal of Nursing Scholarship, 24,* 115–120.

Rodgers, B. L. (1991). Deconstructing the dogma in nursing knowledge and practice. *IMAGE: Journal of Nursing Scholarship, 23,* 177–181.

Wolfer, J. (1993). Aspects of "reality" and ways of knowing in nursing: In search of an integrating paradigm. *IMAGE: Journal of Nursing Scholarship, 25,* 141–146.

6 | SYNTHESIZING KNOWLEDGE AND EXPERIENCE

It is becoming increasingly clear that the human mind and physical universe do not exist independently. Something as yet indefinable connects them. This connective link — between mind and matter, intelligence and intuition — is what Noetic Sciences is all about.

Edgar D. Mitchell, 1973

Daniel and Lyle

Daniel was admitted to a general medical unit of a community hospital for treatment of a chronic back ailment. He was a very successful furniture salesman who traveled frequently. In spite of a promising future in this vocation, which he usually enjoyed very much, at age 34 Daniel was considering a career change. This seemed better to him than the alternative of having to go on disability insurance if his back pain continued to worsen.

Shortly after his admission to the hospital, an evening nurse named Lyle introduced himself to Daniel and they began to talk

about the many concerns that weighed heavily on Daniel's mind. As
he listened to details about his work and family responsibilities, Lyle
carefully assessed Daniel's physical characteristics. In particular, he
noted that his breathing was somewhat labored in spite of clear lung
sounds and no physical exertion. He also noted that Daniel's weight
was at least 50 pounds more than what would be considered "ideal"
for a man of his height.

Lyle used all of his senses (except taste) to complete his assessment of Daniel's physical status. He looked carefully at his skin, hair,
and fingernails. He listened to Daniel's breath and bowel sounds, and
to what he did and did not say. Lyle paid attention to the scent of his
client to determine if any unusual odors were present in any part of
his body. He felt the temperature and texture of Daniel's skin and
palpated the various organs of his abdomen. He also felt the tension
in the muscles of Daniel's neck and back. As he completed his
assessment and began to plan Daniel's nursing care for the evening,
Lyle kept thinking, "This man is just not at ease with himself right
now. He's trying too hard to please someone, so he can't relax and
enjoy his many successes." This thought sort of surprised him
because Daniel's description of his home and work were so positive.
Yet Lyle listened to this inner prompting as he continued with his
evening's work. As bedtime approached, Lyle carefully prepared the
narcotic sedative that Daniel's physician had prescribed. The little
voice within him spoke up again and said, "You know, he might not
really need that medicine. I'll bet he could relax and sleep just fine
with a little help from an intelligent nurse."

As Lyle prepared Daniel for the night's rest, he did not mention
to Daniel that his physician had left the prescribed sleeping medication. Instead, he offered to massage his neck and upper arms. When
Lyle had finished this, Daniel told him how much better he felt and
added, "I had no idea my muscles were so tight." Lyle then asked if
he would like to learn to relax his other major muscles and with his
consent, he taught him a progressive relaxation exercise which Daniel

used successfully in place of sleeping pills for the next 3 nights of his brief hospitalization. During subsequent conversations, Daniel told Lyle how much he appreciated his assistance in learning to relax. The more they talked, the more he began to share his anxieties about not being able to live up to the expectations of his wife and his boss. Daniel began to connect this anxiety to the tension in his neck and back. He agreed to seek further counseling to learn more about how his fears and expectations might be interfering with the structure and functioning of his body.

Daniel's healing was initiated and supported by the intelligent decisions and actions taken by his nurse, Lyle. Lyle's response to Daniel illustrates the nurse's skill in synthesizing knowledge and cognitive awareness about the physical body with intuitive awareness that demanded Lyle's attention in the form of an inner voice. Because Lyle respected his own awareness about Daniel's situation as well as his personal knowledge and intuition based on experience, he offered Daniel an environment in which it was safe for Daniel to increase his awareness for healing.

NOETIC CHARACTERISTICS OF NURSING

The term *noetic* is derived from the Greek word *nous* which means mind, intelligence, or understanding. Noetic refers to use of the intellect or the ability to reason and understand; it is assumed to be the manifestation of a highly developed and organized consciousness. In 1973, Edgar Mitchell, who is quoted in the opening of this chapter, founded the Institute of Noetic Sciences (IONS) as a research foundation and educational institution. For the past 20 years, IONS has been on the cutting edge of interdisciplinary research and education concerning human consciousness. Those who are interested in reading about the research and educational opportunities of this not-for-profit organization can obtain more information by writing to the Institute at 475 Gate Five Road, Suite 300, Sausalito, California 94965.

To be conscious refers to the human ability to be aware of the totality of one's thoughts and feelings, and to be intentional in thinking, feeling, and acting. The anecdote of Daniel and Lyle characterizes nursing as a noetic science. That is, the healing that took place within the context of the nurse-client relationship between Daniel and Lyle is a process in which the nurse uses an awareness of diverse ways of knowing to respond to a patient's unique situation. The nurse's understanding of the intimate relationship between Daniel and the universe prompted him to consider several dimensions of his being to facilitate his healing. Lyle's intelligent responses were not instinctive nor were they readily attributed to knowledge of a particular nursing theory. His plan of care and his actual interventions were more akin to what David Schön (1982) calls "knowing-in-action." Such knowing is dynamic rather than static and is very difficult to verbalize or to put into the formal language of science. It is the personal and tacit knowledge of the expert. Reflecting on one's thoughts and decisions in practice increases the nurse's awareness of what constitutes expert practice. Yet much of the fine detail and differentiation among minute indicators of change often elude the expert in formulating exactly how and what one knows.

Nursing, as a process that facilitates the healing of human beings, rests on an assumption that the one practicing the discipline is conscious and aware of the many types of knowledge and ways of knowing that can be synthesized for the good of the one in need of healing. Nursing science, or the body of knowledge upon which the practice is based, must be intelligent. It must be a noetic science.

Patterns of Knowing

In 1978, Barbara Carper published a synopsis of her dissertation findings about four fundamental patterns of knowing in nursing. Carper asserted that understanding these patterns is essential for the teaching and learning of nursing. The four patterns, which she identified from analyzing the conceptual and syntactical structure of nursing literature, were labeled:

1. Empirics, which is the *science* of nursing

2. Aesthetics, which is the *art* of nursing

3. Personal knowledge, which is the *unique understanding of the individual who practices nursing*

4. Ethics, which is the *moral knowledge of nursing*

Carper's work has been recognized as an original contribution to organizing and understanding the complexity of nursing knowledge. Each of the four patterns contributes to an understanding of the discipline of nursing; none of them alone is sufficient for solving the problems and concerns of the discipline.

When Carper discusses the use of the fundamental patterns of knowing in nursing as a whole, she states, "Nursing thus depends on the specific knowledge of human behavior in health and in illness, the esthetic perception of significant human experiences, a personal understanding of the unique individuality of the self and the capacity to make choices within concrete situations involving particular moral judgments" (p. 23). She adds that each of these interrelated and interdependent patterns should be taught and understood according to its logic, the circumstances in which it is valid, the kinds of data it subsumes, and the methods by which each kind of truth is warranted. To understand the application of these patterns of knowing requires that the nurse develop a keen awareness of each pattern as it influences the nurse's decisions and behaviors toward the client.

The first fundamental pattern of knowing identified by Carper is empirics or the science of nursing. This is knowledge systematically organized into concepts, relational statements, and theories that describe, explain, and predict the scientific phenomena of concern to nursing. Two stages of knowledge development can be identified within this pattern. The first of these is the stage of inquiry known as the "natural history." This stage consists of describing and classifying phenomena that can be known through direct observation and inspection. This type of knowledge can be recognized in nursing education and practice, for example, through physical assessment skills based on knowledge of the sciences of biology and chemistry. Nursing students are taught to use sensory data directly observed, palpated, or heard to construct a diagnostic statement about a patient's actual or potential health problem(s). Following the deductive logic of the scientific method, the student or nurse clinician then proceeds from the diagnostic statement, which links observation with probable etiological cause, to a plan of nursing intervention to prevent or alleviate the patient's problem. Continuing through the deductive process, the nursing intervention is then implemented and evaluated. Outcomes are compared to previous data and stated goals.

The second stage of empirical knowledge development is that of deductively formulated theory. In this stage, nursing goes beyond description and categorization toward the discovery or invention of explanatory models that account for the phenomena previously described and categorized. The second stage of empirics in nursing can be recognized by examining the early theoretical, or grand theory, models in nursing. These models, often fashioned after models from biology and sociology and introduced in chapter 2, included concepts such as adaptation, development, and systems. The objective in developing explanatory models is to move the discipline in the direction of being able to predict and control action that constitutes the practice of nursing. Such empirical knowledge reflects conscious awareness of the physical and social domains of human beings as identified by basic sciences and applied to the practice of nursing. The nurse is aware of concrete facts about a client that can readily be identified by other intelligent persons.

Aesthetic knowledge refers to the artistic aspects of nursing and is explored in more detail in chapter 5. It is expressive and subjective rather than descriptive and objective. Nursing action takes on an aesthetic quality when it goes beyond mere recognition associated with description and categorization, exemplified by the linear nursing process, to perception of the whole. The art of nursing, historically taught as nursing fundamentals, was pushed into the background of curricula and all but disappeared because of the emphasis on empirics and deductive logic in solving the problems of nursing practice. However, there has been a refocusing of nursing curricula on examining the philosophical framework of nursing theories recently and the systematic study of nurses in clinical practice. As a result, the art of nursing is once again identified as an important dimension of this healing discipline. As the nurse, Lyle, demonstrates in the opening vignette of this chapter, his awareness of the total picture, that is, more than Daniel's vital signs and physical symptoms, allowed him to plan and provide healing care.

Carper identifies empathy as a concept that indicates the nurse's application of aesthetic knowing in nursing. Through the experience of empathy, a nurse comes to know the particular experience of the client as that person lives through the experience. Parse's theory of human becoming addresses the importance of the nurse's understanding of the client's personal meanings of health (Parse, 1992). Rather than the nurse acting as an expert judge in identifying the client's health status, the goal of nursing practice is to focus on the lived experience and quality of life of the nurse's client (Cody & Mitchell, 1992). Add to this the nurse's perception of myriad details from the unique environment in which the nurse and client interact and the nurse can then creatively imagine several possible outcomes for nursing care. In relationship with the patient, new meaning and new ways of being are created. The creativity involved in healing is further discussed in chapter 7.

The third pattern of knowing in Carper's view is that of personal knowledge, which she identifies as the most difficult to teach. This is knowing the self and the other in relation to oneself. Authenticity of such knowledge depends on the nurse's willingness to accept another person as is and to recognize that persons (self and other) are constantly changing. This type of knowledge is differentiated from the empirical knowledge needed to manipulate and change the client's environment to facilitate or promote health. Rather, this is a deep recognition and respect for the freedom of each person, nurse and client alike, to be unique and to choose to be in relationships with other free and unique persons. This pattern of knowing in nursing is concerned with a personal encounter between nurse and client in which the wholeness and integrity of each individual is upheld. This requires that the nurse be highly attuned to conscious awareness of self in relation to others. Turning to the opening vignette again, Lyle applied his empirical knowledge in assessing all the physical and psychosocial data he could gather through his senses to formulate a general diagnosis of Daniel's needs for nursing intervention. He also turned inward to pay attention to a personal way of knowing that was familiar to him. His awareness that he could know more about a client than what could be seen, touched, heard, smelled, or tasted meant that Lyle trusted an inner sensing that Daniel was basically strong and healthy. He needed encouragement to become more aware of his own strengths and possibilities.

The fourth and final pattern of knowing identified by Carper is ethics or the moral component. With the increasing complexity of health care, nurses must make difficult decisions about the care they provide to their clients. These decisions must often be made in the face of highly ambiguous and uncertain situations. These decisions often reflect the need to decide between what is right and what is wrong, thus presenting the nurse with a moral dilemma. Carper asserts that the ethical knowledge of nursing focuses on obligation, what ought to be done. Because nursing involves deliberate action toward another person, principles used in making judgments about that action may come into conflict. Ethical knowledge, then, concerns the judgment made in a concrete situation about the action to be taken by the nurse. Mere knowledge of ethical codes or standards of care provides a framework for this, but ethical choices also depend on the nurse's understanding of the philosophical frameworks and assumptions behind principles guiding the judgments made. To act on ethical knowledge requires that the nurse be aware of his values and beliefs, biases and skepticisms. The nurse must acknowledge that personal preferences and priorities may be in conflict with those of the client, the client's family, or other members of the health care team. An in-depth discussion of nursing ethics is beyond the scope of this book. However, developing the nurse's awareness of ethical conflicts and behaviors is essential to the healing of clients and the reader is encouraged to delve more deeply into this important component of nursing practice and decision making.

Nursing Process

The nursing process is a method used by nurses to solve problems in giving nursing care. It is a framework for professional nursing practice (Chitty, 1993). The nursing process is a method or tool for nursing professionals and helps them to arrive at decisions, and to predict and evaluate consequences. It is a deliberate intellectual activity enabling the nurse to practice in an orderly, systematic, and predictable manner. Rew and Barrow argue that although the five steps of assessment, diagnosis, planning, implementation, and evaluation suggest a forward movement through each discrete phase, this does not necessarily happen in practice. The nursing process has been a focal point in teaching novice nurses the knowledge and skills deemed essential for safe nursing practice.

The nursing process is familiar because it is a variant of the step-by-step scientific method or problem-solving algorithm. As noted by Rew and Barrow (1989), "the nursing process describes a downhill flow" (p. 356). To be successful, each step of this linear process depends on the success of each preceding step. When an error or oversight occurs in the first step of assessing the sensory data from the client, each succeeding step in the nursing process reflects that error. The process is based on the rules of deductive logic and forms the basis of fundamental education in nursing. Historically, it has provided a comforting and necessary structure for organizing and educating professional nurses. Its strength lies in its ability to provide a sound framework for solving simple problems in nursing care. However, when sensory data are changing rapidly or are ambiguous, uncertain, or conflicting, such a structured process is inadequate for solving the complex problems of planning and providing nursing care.

Based on Aristotelian logic and the philosophy of empiricism, nursing education and practice have organized much knowledge around the steps of the nursing process. For example, assessment of the physical and mental status of human beings is considered essential content in professional nursing curricula. Similarly, formulation of appropriate nursing diagnoses with identifying characteristics and etiological factors also comprises much of the knowledge presented to fledgling practitioners. Current efforts abound in nursing research to identify specific interventions, to classify them into a taxonomy, and to establish evidence that their use leads to desirable outcomes in nursing clients. This focus has resulted in a distorted awareness among many nurses as the only pattern of nursing knowledge that is worthy of expression in clinical practice.

Reliance on the linear nursing process, as described in basic nursing textbooks, limits the practice of nursing to predictable behaviors based on the accurate adherence to the rules of deductive logic. Such limitations have contributed to the recent exodus of nurses who left the discipline because they were "fed up, fearful, and frazzled" (Gorman, 1988, pp. 77–78). Taken to its extreme, imagine what nursing would be like if it reached "the ultimate in scientific development," if nursing behaviors were completely predictable and controllable. Nursing care (behaviors) could be provided by a team of highly skilled, intelligent, and friendly computerized robots. Perfect in every conceivable way, they could speak, deliver medications and other treatments, and collect and record empirical evidence of vital signs and symptoms.

A programmed robot could enter a hospitalized client's room precisely on schedule to deliver meals, to collect the trays after meals are completed, and to accurately document the quantity and caloric value of all food and beverages consumed. Such a robot could deliver to the client and the client's physician a detailed account of the appropriate nursing diagnoses based on the client's history and the data gathered and recorded from the day's process of monitoring empirical indicators. Robots could replace the nurse if the process of providing nursing care were only the accurate gathering of data, formulating diagnostic statements, prescribing and implementing interventive behaviors, and evaluating outcomes. Fortunately for the discipline and for our clients, nursing is much more than that.

While efforts to organize and structure nursing knowledge have done much to advance nursing as a science, much of the intelligence expressed by the nursing expert defies description and classification. Recent research in nursing and other fields such as women's studies and information systems provides additional ways to conceptualize knowledge and its thoughtful application in the human noetic science of healing.

WOMEN'S KNOWING

Much of what is known and taught about thinking, reasoning, and knowing has come from research conducted by men about men. For example, Lawrence Kohlberg's (1981) work on moral reasoning spawned a great deal of research and found that women often did not "measure up" to males in selecting the "right" answer for moral situations. In 1982, Harvard researcher Carol Gilligan published the findings of three research investigations she carried out to explore the language and logic used by women. The first study was about the identity and moral development of 25 college female students. The second study was done with 24 women and concerned the decision-making process related to having an abortion. The third study included males and females, matched for age and other sociocultural demographic factors. This study of 144 persons explored the different modes of thinking about morality that resulted from analysis of data in the first two studies.

Gilligan's findings in these three studies are beginning to change the way we think about ethics and moral decision making. They provide evidence that boys and girls, men and women, think differently about how to solve dilemmas based on the values they hold about the world and the people and situations in it. For example, Gilligan notes that males and females experience different dynamics in the processes of separation from and attachment to other people. For males, separation brings identity and power, whereas for females attachment sustains the feelings of connection and community that are of utmost importance. These findings add to our understanding of what might go into the healing of persons who are clients of the nurse. For women, according to Gilligan's findings, identity of self is bound into the context of relationships, thus healing for women must take this fundamental characteristic into consideration. In contrast, for men, identity of self is defined more by characteristics that separate them from others, thus their uniqueness and individuality are important aspects of healing.

Information Systems

The introduction of computer technology into the health care industry has enabled nurses and other health care professionals to streamline communication, reduce errors in routine tasks, and open the way for new ways of looking at old problems. One aspect of the science of information systems that holds exciting possibilities for nursing and other disciplines devoted to the healing of persons and the environment is that of fuzzy logic.

Fuzzy logic refers to a process of knowing and making decisions based on vagueness and uncertainty (Rew, Waller, & Barrow, 1994). The processes that take place between persons during healing are not discrete phenomena that are easily measured and quantified. When studied systematically, these phenomena tend to be characterized as continuous, rather than interval- or ratio-type, variables. The usual binary logic used by computers and in statistical analysis of variables limits the interpretation of data of interest to nurses. Traditional binary logic and statistical inference addresses hypotheses that are either true or false, represented by a "1" or a "0" (Stewart, 1993). Statistical analyses performed by modern computers are based on the laws of probability that a statement is either true or it is not true. Many statements about humans may be partly true and partly not true. Hence, fuzzy logic can assist in analyzing the gray areas between black and white or between true and false. Programmed with fuzzy logic, computers can deal with concepts such as sore or soft and measure the degree to which a certain condition exists for an individual (Kosko & Isaka, 1993).

The usefulness of nursing interventions to promote healing has been studied using traditional logic and statistical analyses. Many important and significant results have been obtained. However, many situations do not readily lend themselves to such mathematical models, and fuzzy logic as a component of information systems may find a place in future research on human healing. The reader interested in learning more about fuzzy logic will find additional entries in the Annotated Bibliography at the end of this book.

KNOWING IN HEALING

What is needed in situations of great uncertainty and ambiguity is a complex process of human consciousness that allows and enables the nurse to be aware of and draw on all of the formal and informal knowledge, beliefs, and experiences to synthesize the many ways of knowing into action that is appropriate for complex and expert nursing care. This process is nonlinear, intuitive, and dialectical and, until recently, it has been largely ignored or disdained by mainstream nursing education. However, today there is a growing body of research literature to support the claim that this process is not only appropriate, but that it is alive and well in the ranks of nursing practitioners.

Marlaine Smith (1992) states, "Knowing is a holistic and integrative process of making sense out of ourselves in our world" (p. 2). She states that personal knowing is primary to all the other ways of knowing. She adds that the judgments we make are personal, reflecting our values and views of the world. If this is true, then it is imperative that those who are nurses be very much aware of themselves. It may be essential to know oneself very well before one can really know another person. David Bohm, a theoretical physicist, reflects on the paradoxical nature of human knowledge when he states that the more science learns, the more the mystery of the nature of the universe grows (Weber, 1986). He goes on to add, "The awareness of the unity and interconnectedness of all being leads — if it is consistent — to an empathy with others. It expresses itself as reverence for life, compassion, a sense of the brotherhood of suffering humanity and the commitment to heal our wounded earth and its peoples" (p. 21).

Nursing as a noetic human science requires that its practitioners and scholars gather, organize, synthesize, and apply all patterns of knowing in ways that facilitate the healing of persons. Such complex behavior begins with the clinician's awareness of an intelligent unity of which both nurse and client are components. This awareness of connection between persons and its relationship to healing is reflected by Philip Goldberg (1983) who writes, "We protect and nurture that which we perceive as part of ourselves, but the sense of connection with people and nature has to be deeply felt, not just thought about" (p. 215).

Nursing as a healing discipline has amassed an impressive body of knowledge that includes empirical data, personal knowledge, aesthetics, ethics, and intuition. Together, these patterns of knowing, including some yet to be named, represent a noetic science. These are ways of knowing that cannot merely be memorized and automatically applied to predictable situations. As illustrated in the vignette of Daniel and Lyle, the nurse was aware of the diversity of his ways of knowing and felt deeply about Daniel's problems and potentials. Trusting in the process of connected healing between them, he was able to plan and implement nursing care that was highly individualized and beneficial to them both. Lyle was also able to take a risk and reject an option, the hypnotic drug, that could have acted as a barrier to healing.

References

Carper, B. A. (1978). Fundamental patterns of knowing in nursing. *Advances in Nursing Science, 1* (1), 13–23.

Chitty, K. K. (1993). *Professional nursing: Concepts and challenges.* Philadelphia: W. B. Saunders Company.

Cody, W. K., & Mitchell, G. J. (1992). Parse's theory as a model for practice: The cutting edge. *Advances in Nursing Science, 15* (2), 52–65.

Gilligan, C. (1982). *In a different voice.* Cambridge, MA: Harvard University Press.

Goldberg, P. (1983). *The intuitive edge.* Los Angeles: Jeremy Tarcher, Inc.

Gorman, C. (1988, March 14). Fed up, fearful, and frazzled. *Time,* pp. 77–78.

Kohlberg, L. (1981). *The philosophy of moral development.* San Francisco: Harper and Row.

Kosko, B., & Isaka, S. (1993, July). Fuzzy logic. *Scientific American,* pp. 76–81.

Mitchell, E. (1973). Promotional materials for the Institute of Noetic Sciences. (Available from the Institute of Noetic Sciences, 475 Gate Five Rd., Ste. 300, Sausalito, CA 94965)

Parse, R. R. (1992). Human becoming: Parse's theory of nursing. *Nursing Science Quarterly, 5,* 35–42.

Rew, L., & Barrow, E. M. (1989). Nurses' intuition: Can it coexist with the nursing process? *Association of Operating Room Nurses Journal, 50,* 353–358.

Rew, L., Waller, P. R., & Barrow, E. M. (1994). Fuzzy logic: Enhancing possibilities for nursing intervention research. In P. L. Chinn (Ed.), *Advances in Methods of inquiry for Nursing* (pp. 32–40). Gaithersburg, MD: Aspen Publishers, Inc.

Schön, D. A. (1982). *The reflective practitioner.* Basic Books.

Smith, M. C. (1992). Is all knowing personal knowing? *Nursing Science Quarterly, 5* (1), 2–3.

Stewart, I. (1993). Mathematical recreations: A partly true story. *Scientific American, 268* (2), 110–112.

Weber, R. (1986). Renee Weber interviews David Bohm. *Noetic Sciences Review,* Winter, 20–21.

Suggested Reading

Gordon, M., Murphy, C. P., & Candee, D. (1994). Clinical judgment: An integrated model. *Advances in Nursing Science, 16* (4), 55–70.

Schlotfeldt, R. M. (1988). Structuring nursing knowledge: A priority for creating nursing's future. *Nursing Science Quarterly, 1,* 35–38.

Schön, D. (1987). *Educating the reflective practitioner.* San Francisco: Jossey-Bass Publishers.

Slobodkin, L. B. (1992). *Simplicity and complexity in games of the intellect.* Cambridge, MA: Harvard University Press.

7 CREATIVITY AND HEALING AWARENESS

*As healing awareness develops one learns to witness
the content, process and context of consciousness,
without trying to evaluate, control, or modify them.*

F. Vaughan, 1986

Jared, Teresa, and Mary

The young mother stood quietly next to the hospital bed where her young son lay. She gently stroked the curly blond locks away from his fevered brow and sponged the feverish perspiration with a soft cloth. In spite of her outward appearance of calm control, her heart was heavy with concern about the fate of this precious five-year-old. Thoughts and feelings raced through her mind as she considered the outcome of the examination of Jared's spinal fluid. "Could it be meningitis? Will he die? Will he recover but have neurological damage? I'm so scared. . . . What about the younger children at home? Have they been exposed to this frightening germ also? I feel so helpless right now. . . . How will we manage if I have to quit working to stay home and care for Jared? What will this do to our marriage? I feel so alone right now. . . . Where is Kurt when I really need him?"

Jared's nurse, Mary, came by his bedside to assess his temperature and check the status of the intravenous fluids dripping into the small arm of her young patient. She observed Teresa's gentle demeanor with Jared and said to her, "Teresa, you must be feeling exhausted by now. Would it help if I brought you a cup of tea and we could sit together with Jared for a while?" Teresa looked up at the nurse with a reluctant smile and slowly nodded her head.

Mary brought Teresa the tea and sat down with her for a few minutes. She asked Teresa about the other members of her family and laughed with her as they talked about the funny things that happen when small children run about. Mary skillfully directed Teresa's attention away from her worries and toward thoughts of more pleasant experiences. Mary shared some of her own experiences as a mother of two young children and how they sometimes caused headaches in their parents, but most of the time they were a great source of entertainment and joy. Mary also asked Teresa about the activities she enjoyed when she wasn't busy caring for her children. She discovered that she and Teresa had a mutual interest in cross-stitching and she encouraged Teresa to bring some of her work into the hospital the next time she came for a visit.

Two days later, Jared was watching television and eating a popsicle when Mary came by to check his temperature. Teresa was again sitting at Jared's bedside. This time she was quietly counting the cross-stitches on a small picture. She stood as the nurse went to Jared's side and she said, "Mary, thank you so much for your time and the tea on Sunday night. I guess I didn't realize how frightened I was and how much I might be hindering Jared's recovery with my own thoughts and feelings. You really helped me to put that all into perspective and now look how well he's doing!"

The vignette about Jared, Teresa, and Mary illustrates how an expert nurse blended her knowledge and experience to intervene in a creative manner for healing. Few nursing textbooks describe in detail the process Mary used in planning and intervening to assist Jared in this healing experience. The illustration is rich with data from which one could draw inferences and plan nursing care based on the probable causes and outcomes of Jared's medical condition using the usual problem-solving steps of the nursing process. But Mary trusted her personal knowledge and intuition combined with many previous nursing experiences with children and their parents to guide her in spontaneously offering an intervention that enabled Teresa to focus awareness on her motivations and behaviors toward Jared. This chapter addresses the creative application of knowledge in establishing a healing environment.

CREATIVE APPLICATION OF KNOWLEDGE

In the previous chapter, the nurse's synthesis of applied knowledge from basic sciences and the humanities with personal knowledge, intuition, and experience was identified as a vehicle for healing. In this chapter, creativity is discussed as another dimension of nursing intervention to promote healing. In addition to the use of critical thinking skills, problem solving in nursing often involves going beyond the boundaries of traditional solutions and having the courage to look at circumstances from a different perspective.

Healing is not merely restoration or return to a previous health state. Rather, it is a new awareness that is created out of breakdown in the natural wholeness and harmony between a person and the universe. It is an act of creation. The story of Jared and his mother, Teresa, sounds amazingly simple and straightforward. It sounds like a generic example of the natural healing that occurs with the passage of time with no particular or intentional intervention from others. It also appears that Jared's recovery was evidenced by a return to a previous level of physical activity and health as shown in his eating the popsicle and watching television. The healing that took place in this story, however, has another dimension that was recognized by Mary, the nurse. That dimension is the healing awareness that took place in Jared's mother. Teresa was so tuned in to her own anxiety and distress that she unknowingly interfered with a supportive and healing environment for her son. The presence of anxious family members is a common context in which children struggle through illnesses and diseases. Reducing the response to stress and anxiety among parents becomes a challenge for creative interventions by the nurse. Creativity begins with awareness that something new is needed. The nurse who is aware of many possible solutions to problems has creativity as an ally. This means awareness of realities that exist beyond what is apparent through the external appearance of things.

Jacob Needleman (1993), a professor of philosophy, suggests that the only way to know the world that is behind external appearances is to look inward. Things are not always as they look from the outside. The process of looking inward leads to a heightened sense of self-awareness. With this increase in self-awareness comes a greater appreciation of how our thoughts and behaviors alter the environment around us. Frances Vaughan (1986), a psychotherapist, states that the conscious process of developing a sense of wholeness begins with self-consciousness and continues through further exploration of the world within. She adds that this process of awakening awareness of the universe within is healing.

In the illustration of Jared and Teresa, Mary recognized that Teresa's anxiety formed a barrier to Jared's healing. This recognition on Mary's part might have reflected basic knowledge of human psychology and behavior or it might have reflected personal knowledge based on years of experience with similar patterns of behavior that she had observed between parents and children. Mary's intervention reflected not only this knowledge and experience, but an awareness of the importance of her own presence in creating a healing environment.

Mary intervened first by focusing on Teresa's need for rest, comfort, and diversion. Mary did not remove Teresa from the environment, but redirected the focus of Teresa's concern about her son to recognition of her own needs and the restoration of energy that she would need to help Jared. Mary creatively transformed the sick room into a tea party where Teresa's physical and emotional needs could be met. Mary not only brought a hot cup of comforting tea to Teresa, but she took the time to find some pretty napkins and a small fresh flower to place on the tray that she brought with her to Jared's room.

Mary's intervention is an example of the creative thinking that has long been a tradition in nursing care. Creative thinking is based on an open attitude that allows the nurse to play with knowledge and experience to find new and individualized ways to promote the healing process. This type of thinking and problem solving is characterized by flexibility and originality. It involves looking for relationships between ideas or things that are not obvious or that have not been tried before. Many strategies exist to help nurses exercise and improve their creative problem solving. One way is to participate in group brainstorming where a large number of solutions to a problem are generated without judgment or rules governing their feasibility. Later these solutions can be evaluated in terms of their practicality. Pesut (1985) also advocates "thinking about thinking" as a means for tapping into creative solutions. In other words, creative problem solving is the result of paying attention to our thoughts and trying new ways of looking at our responses rather than continuously responding in ritualistic or habitual ways. Nurses' strict adherence to following the five steps of the nursing process can become habituated and responses to unique situations presented by clients are easily ignored. By engaging in thinking about the steps of the process, innovative solutions can be applied.

Clients can also be stimulated to engage in creative problem solving as part of the healing process. Divergent thinking involves taking a different path toward a goal; it involves tolerance for ambiguity and entertaining the possibility that there are multiple solutions rather than just one right answer. This type of activity may result in new awarenesses about hidden talents and potentials within an individual that can be used for healing. One suggestion for assisting clients to identify new response patterns is to have them generate lists of alternative activities for reaching goals (McClam & Woodside, 1994). The same principles followed in group brainstorming apply: allow the imagination to run wild and identify as many activities as come to mind, regardless of how impractical or foolish they may appear. Moving from possibilities to choices empowers individuals to get what they really want (Egan, 1994). This process enables people to move from a position of being stuck into the light of new freedom, which in itself may have a healing effect.

Roger von Oech (1990), president of a business consulting firm called Creative Think, states that a creative outlook enables a person to explore new possibilities and to change situations that need to be changed. He identifies a number of reasons why people are not creative in their thinking. These include the rigid adherence to rules, doubting that a new idea will work because it is impractical or illogical, the fear of being wrong, and the belief that play is frivolous.

Creative Healing in Life Transitions

Creative interventions are a daily component of expert nursing practice. They are apparent in small gestures such as bringing tea to an exhausted young mother. Some healing interventions require even more creativity, especially when medical and nursing science seem to have little else to offer to clients. This type of creativity is called for in end-of-life transitions where curing is no longer probable, but healing is still needed. The following vignette shows the creative response of a nurse in such a situation.

Julia and Barbara

Julia was only 34 years of age when she learned that the discomfort in her abdomen was due to the presence of a malignant tumor — "a silly melanoma," as she called it. Julia's life had been anything but simple up to this point and the diagnosis crashed into her family like one more wave on a stormy sea. During the months of treatments with short reprieves from her suffering, Julia worried about her three young children and her loving husband who seemed so devastated by the thought of losing her. She knew she had to be strong for all of them, but what about the anger and resentment she felt? What about the feelings that this was just a bit too much?

Julia was a psychotherapist herself and well-versed in the theories of stress and grief. She knew that psychological theorists had claimed that people could find meaning in their suffering. She knew that these experts and scholars had claimed that people could transcend bad experiences and connect to a larger view of their lives, not be controlled by the circumstances of an unfair present. Intellectually, Julia knew there was hope for her in this hopeless condition, but emotionally her fears and anger prevented her from approaching this crisis as an opportunity rather than a danger.

A colleague of Julia's, a nurse-psychotherapist named Barbara, began to visit her and to suggest a creative new way of looking at her predicament. After several heart-to-heart talks, Barbara presented Julia with the following story:

"The Creation and Purpose of Millie Noma"

Millie was created but she had no clue as to why. Her personality was unpredictable at best and her behavior was erratic. She usually ended up wandering aimlessly around somebody else's body in search of why she was there. She didn't feel particularly welcome anywhere that she went. Sometimes she would establish her home out-of-doors only to be told that she was ugly and didn't belong there. She would then wiggle deep into a dark and damp cave. Nobody wanted her to set up housekeeping there either. Her hosts and hostesses were constantly hurling daggers and poisons at her. Yet, she went on and on and on.

One day Millie met a friend. This friend was of superior intelligence and compassion. This friend listened patiently to Millie's story. The friend nodded sympathetically as Millie poured out her tales of woe. She was an immature, formless being with no appealing identifying features. Nobody liked her, yet she had survived numerous attempts to capture and eradicate her. Millie's new friend made no judgments about those who did not welcome Millie into their "homes." Millie's new friend merely told her that she did belong in the world and that she was created for a purpose. Millie's friend pointed out how strong she was and how clever she was to continue living in spite of all those other creatures who treated her as an unwanted foreigner and tried to shove her out.

Millie listened carefully to this new friend. She thought about how ungrateful she had been for her life and how thoughtless she had been about intruding into the lives of these other creatures without so much as their permission, much less their invitation to "move in." She realized that the more she felt unwelcome in a new host's "home," the more she got riled up and demanded even more living space. Her fear of becoming extinct was so enormous that she became very spoiled, insisting on only the best living quarters and dining experiences. She had completely lost sight of the fact that she had been created to teach human beings about living and about loving. That was a pretty awesome reason for being.

Her friend helped her to see that she could be almost as lovable as a teddy bear. If she remembered her Creator and her Purpose, she could teach her hosts and hostesses and they could learn about the reasons why they were created. But this was a difficult task and she didn't have many skills. She decided that she just wanted and needed some attention. She knew that her life would be short and pretty insignificant compared to those she chose to "visit." After all, they were the really strong and intelligent beings. Yet, she wanted to be loved and accepted for who she was and for what she was capable of doing. She wanted some old-fashioned, honest-to-goodness respect! Her new friend suggested that perhaps if she would go about her daily life a bit more calmly she could earn that respect. She might be welcome for a short while, until she had imparted the lesson for which she had been created, but then she would have to be willing to move on. Millie thought about all the new things she was hearing from her new friend. It made her feel better.

Millie Noma was a curious little creature. Sometimes she looked and acted just like a teddy bear, but it often seemed like her heart was in the wrong place. Life was hard for her because she couldn't see where she was going or what she was doing. She usually just pushed and kicked her way around, trying to define herself and feel comfortable. She took advantage of the nicest people on earth and made them miserable at times.

If you find Millie on your journey through life, remember her purpose. She can show you your strength and she can help you feel all the love that is in and around you. But she needs help in remembering her place in the great scheme of things. So, if you see her, remember that she hears you but can't see you. Tell her what you think and feel about her visit to you. Then, when you are ready, put her in a safe place, thank her, and tell her that her mission has been accomplished!

Barbara made a little patchwork teddy bear in Julia's favorite colors and gave it to her after writing the story. At the time of this visit, Barbara knew that Julia could not read the story, so she told her the main points of it while Julia held the little bear. Julia laughed and began to beat Millie on the kitchen counter saying, "Millie, get in your place." Then she hugged the little bear and Barbara and said how good it felt to be loved and cared for. One week later Julia died in her sleep.

Barbara creatively intervened by using her imagination and humor to engage in healing at this end-of-life transition. She acknowledged that the cancer was incurable but recognized the importance of giving Julia one more chance to express her anger and disappointment with the condition of her body. The intervention was healing for Barbara as well because it gave her the sense that in what might otherwise seem a hopeless situation, there was another way of looking at Julia's illness.

Vaughan (1986) states that healing awareness can be evoked in others by an individual who consciously models it. Barbara's behavior reflected an attitude of acceptance of life transitions. Her specific intervention is what Helen Erickson, a nurse theorist, and her colleagues call *the art of modeling* the client's world (Erickson, Tomlin, & Swain, 1983). The art of modeling requires creativity and communication skills to develop a mirror image of the client's situation from that individual's unique perspective.

Creativity invites us to turn old beliefs and habits upside down. In so doing, we may gain new insights about healing and living. These insights are part of developing awareness about what contributes to healing and what hinders the process. This book represents a creative approach to developing both the nurse's and the client's awareness. It includes many traditional values and facts that nurses have used in their healing practices for years. The next and final chapter offers a variety of exercises to enhance awareness and creativity.

Healing can never be reduced to a predictable science. It will always require a measure of creativity to be relevant to an individual's experience and unique place in the universe. It can be promoted and facilitated by increasing self-awareness within the client and within the client's nurse or other helping person. There is no one right way to do this. Each client's situation is unique and each nurse-client relationship is novel. Healing depends on acknowledgment of the highly individualized meaning that persons make of their experiences. Those who hope to contribute to the healing of persons, either themselves or others, must be willing to take a creative approach.

The vignettes at the beginning of each chapter in this book are examples of the creative application of knowledge, experience, and awareness for healing. All of them are based on real clients and their nurses although their names and demographic details have been altered to protect their identities. In chapter 1 the nurse, Clara, reflected on Sally's sad countenance following her surgery for a malignant melanoma and placed this observed facial expression within the metaphor of a hazy cocoon where Sally was suspended. From this model of the client's world, Clara decided how to intervene in a way that could gently release Sally from a trap and enable her to re-emerge into the world as a creation of beauty (much like a butterfly). Clara's interventions, which included Sally's use of various senses and modalities such as crying, listening, drawing, and writing, increased Sally's awareness of a healing process within her. Clara stimulated Sally's awareness by helping her to remove barriers associated with blocked emotions about memories from childhood. With explanations from Clara about the beliefs Sally had about herself and the way her body responded to her internal messages, Sally developed a cognitive awareness of how the several dimensions of herself were interconnected. She also learned to trust her inner feelings and explore other meaningful relationships that could facilitate her healing. This intuitive awareness contributed to her renewed enjoyment in being with other people and learning to trust them in new ways. Over time, Clara also assisted Sally in creating new meaning and purpose in her life. Freed from the barriers she had imposed on herself through limited beliefs and expectations about herself, Sally gradually developed a respect and interest in the spiritual dimension of her life. Through transcendent awareness, she finally experienced a measure of peace about her past and looked forward to raising her children while enjoying a new appreciation for her body, mind, and soul.

In chapter 2, Joshua's camp nurse, Cheryl, provided a creative intervention with Joshua's mother by sharing her eclectic philosophy of self-care and health promotion for children. The application of an eclectic philosophy fulfills the criteria of creative problem solving. That is, there is not a rigid adherence to a single ideology or method. The nurse with this type of philosophy has a mind that is open to new possibilities and is eager to entertain putting new ideas together in novel and interesting ways. Consequently, many more solutions can be generated.

Camp nursing resonates with creative interventions and lends itself naturally to including aesthetics in the healing environment. The entire context for interacting with clients is filled with endless opportunities. The usual parameters of the nurse-client relationship within a highly structured health care setting are missing in this type of setting and nurses can observe and interact with their clients in a more natural environment that is conducive to building awareness for healing. Many of the barriers that exist in other institutions such as schools, hospitals, and doctors' offices are not present in the outdoor setting of camp. This type of setting often enhances and reinforces intuitive and transcendent awareness. Continuous interaction with nature — listening to its sounds, taking in the aromas, and observing the natural rhythms of wind blowing the grass and trees — all stimulate the mind to consider the interconnectedness of all life. This awareness has facilitated healing throughout history and across all cultures.

Harriet's nurse, Ann, in chapter 3, recognized that her client had literally translated her feelings into a somatic problem: her husband Jonathan turned her stomach! Through creative intervention, Ann assisted Harriet in identifying the barriers to healing that she had erected. Energy that Harriet could have used creatively was turned instead into a destructive physical process that was robbing her of time and personal fulfillment. As Harriet paid more attention to her inner voice and the wisdom that it carried, she developed intuitive awareness that contributed to her healing. Ann worked first through cognitive awareness to help her identify the factors that supported her illness and as Harriet acknowledged these factors in a cognitive way, she also realized that her body was responding intelligently to her inner wisdom telling her that the situation was sickening. This intuitive awareness served as a lifesaver for Harriet.

Similarly, Mindy, the skinny kid who was unaware that she was starving herself to death, presented in chapter 4, was using her energy toward a destructive end. However, with Beverly's creative care that connected the aesthetics of sensory experience with emotion through Mindy's drawing of the mouse eating the big strawberry, Mindy became aware of her view of the world around her, including her fear of growing up and adopting the role of a mature woman. Beverly helped her translate symbols of her fears and views into more concrete forms that she could then think about changing. Mindy's illness of anorexia was very complex and the starvation of her body acted as a resistant barrier to developing awareness. Through the use of aesthetics, Beverly touched an inner, intuitive awareness within Mindy that was then used to help her focus on the cognitive awareness she would need to take concrete action to help herself.

Jane's story of shielding herself from the pain of an ankle injury, presented in chapter 5, does not illustrate a creative intervention from a nurse. However, Jane's construction and application of personal and intuitive knowledge for healing are examples of creativity and strategies for self-healing. They represent uniqueness and spontaneity, which are also hallmarks of creativity. As such, they are essential to developing the fullest awareness needed for healing. Jane already had a well-developed cognitive awareness of the intimate relationship between her body and mind and trusted her intuitive awareness to simplify the healing process.

Lyle, Daniel's nurse in chapter 6, demonstrates a nurse's willingness to trust and act on personal and intuitive knowledge. Lyle listens to his own inner voice in addition to thinking analytically about the data he collected through his other senses. His actions chosen to help Daniel with his back pain are not based on a fear of being wrong about withholding sleeping medication nor of thinking that his inner voice was illogical or impractical. Rather they reflect Lyle's synthesis of cognitive and intuitive awareness. The nurse who begins with personal knowledge about his own dimensions of awareness can then be empathic with clients whose healing processes can be promoted through developing their levels of awareness.

As noted earlier in this chapter, Mary blended her cognitive and personal knowledge and previous nursing experience to intervene creatively with Jared and his mother, Teresa. Each of these nurses provides a glimpse of the creative application of diverse ways of knowing that characterizes nursing. Each exemplifies at least one dimension of awareness that contributes to the healing of the individual client within his unique set of circumstances. This type of response does not emulate a single grand theory of nursing. Creating awareness imitates the consciousness that is needed for healing. If nurses believe that the nature of the universe is one of wholeness and harmony, then they will respond in creative and exciting new ways to each client they meet.

References

Egan, G. (1994). *The skilled helper* (5th ed.). Pacific Grove, CA: Brooks/Cole Publishing Company.

Erickson, H. C., Tomlin, E. M., & Swain, M. A. P. (1983). *Modeling and role-modeling.* Englewood Cliffs, NJ: Prentice-Hall, Inc.

McClam, T., & Woodside, M. (1994). *Problem solving in the helping professions.* Pacific Grove, CA: Brooks/Cole Publishing Company.

Needleman, J. (1993, Summer). Questions of the heart. *Noetic Sciences Review, 26,* 4–9.

Pesut, D. (1985). Toward a new definition of creativity. *Nurse Educator, 10,* 5.

Vaughan, F. (1986). *The inward arc.* Boston: New Science Library.

von Oech, R. (1990). *A whack on the side of the head: How you can be more creative.* New York: Warner Books.

Suggested Reading

Anderson, W. (1992). The great memory. *Noetic Sciences Review, 21,* 21–28.

Moyers, B. (1989). *A world of ideas.* New York: Doubleday.

Moyers, B. (1990). *A world of ideas, II.* New York: Doubleday.

FROM COGNITIVE TO TRANSCENDENT AWARENESS

8

*In that strange state of consciousness when the heart
is reaching and thought has frayed out to thin,
unimportant stuff without any form, a shutter of
the soul sometimes springs open and fixes an image
for an instant.*

V. B. Tower, 1987

Bessie and Margaret

Bessie was 74 years old when she met Margaret, her husband's nurse.
Bessie was a devoted wife and mother who had spent over 50 years
creating a cozy home for her husband and their four daughters. Now
George was very ill and Bessie felt helpless and frightened. Margaret
provided the highest standard of nursing care to George, keeping him
clean and comfortable for his final transition in living. She knew that
her actions toward George were important to ease his transition. She
also knew that every little thing she did was under constant scrutiny
by Bessie and her four daughters (Rita, Vera, Ettiene, and Ruth).

Margaret took extra time to describe to George, who was slowly slipping into a coma, all that she was doing for him and why. Bessie, Rita, Vera, Ettiene, and Ruth also heard every word Margaret said and would sometimes stop her and ask for a fuller explanation of why she was doing a specific task.

During the short week of George's hospitalization, Margaret took more and more time to include Bessie, Rita, Vera, Ettiene, and Ruth in providing George's nursing care. She encouraged these women to talk to George, to tell him things they always wanted him to know, and to participate in comforting him by washing his face and brushing his hair. She watched and listened carefully to the ways they interacted as a family. She began to recognize Bessie's fear of being left alone and feeling ill-equipped to manage the family finances. She asked if Bessie would be willing to talk with a social worker about her future plans. Bessie declined. On the day before George's death, however, Bessie asked Margaret if she would continue to be *her* nurse after George was gone. Although this wasn't in her job description, Margaret listened to her inner wisdom and answered Bessie with an enthusiastic, "Yes, of course. Please call me any time."

For the next 2 years, Bessie and Margaret met twice monthly in Bessie's home. What happened during and between those visits exemplifies the three types of awareness discussed in this book. At first, Bessie was unaware of the normal grieving process. She wanted information about how she was supposed to act and feel. Her daughters often presented barriers to her healing as she grieved long and hard for George; they wanted desperately for her "to get on with her life"; to adjust, to find new friends and maybe even a new husband! But Bessie had spent most of her life with George and she needed more time to assimilate the loss. She discovered that much of her personal identity as well as her social connections had come from her relationship with him. She hardly knew who she was or could be, only what she should be as George's wife and the mother of George's four daughters.

As Bessie and Margaret worked through the cognitive awareness of this great change in Bessie's life, Bessie also became aware of her personal perceptions of the world. She began to understand that as her relationship with George grew over the years she had often been able to know what he wanted or needed without even asking him. She had not previously considered that this intuitive awareness was a part of what helped her feel close and connected to him. As Margaret helped her to explore this, Bessie began to see that this intuitive awareness gave her life meaning and purpose and now that George was no longer there, she wondered how her life could ever have meaning and purpose again. Margaret showed her that George wasn't the only person with whom Bessie had strong connections and that intuitive awareness could help her re-evaluate her other important relationships with family members and friends.

One day Bessie called Margaret and asked if she could come for a visit that same afternoon. On the phone she told Margaret that she had had a very unusual experience and she wanted to make sure she wasn't going crazy. Margaret was off-duty that day, so late in the afternoon she drove over to Bessie's apartment. They talked for a few minutes and then Bessie said she had felt George's presence in their living room that morning. She said that she was watching television and suddenly a tremendous calm came over her. Bessie added, "I felt like he was right there telling me that everything was going to be all right." On the one hand, Bessie felt relief that she had experienced this calm feeling and reassurance from her beloved George. On the other hand, she had never experienced anything like this before in her lifetime. She was afraid that it meant she was losing her mind!

Margaret and Bessie considered these two possibilities. Margaret asked Bessie several other questions to assess her mental abilities and found no other signs that Bessie was losing her ability to perceive reality. Bessie agreed that she was still well-oriented to time, place, and person. Then Margaret asked Bessie to imagine what it would be like to be over her sadness and depression about George's loss. She had previously taught Bessie progressive relaxation exercises with guided imagery to help her handle the hassles of everyday living. Bessie closed her eyes, sat back in her rocker, and began to rock back and forth in her comfortable old chair. After a few minutes, she slowly started to smile and nod her head. She said to Margaret, "Well, you know, I guess I would finally know that George wasn't really gone and that he's still very much alive in my memory."

Bessie's final realization is an example of transcendent awareness. She knew that her bond with George went beyond time and physical parameters. She understood that in spite of his being gone, her life retained purpose and meaning and that he was still a big part of that. She realized that her healing and recovery from the trauma of losing George had happened through her gradual awareness of the many dimensions and complexities of her life. Margaret, as a skilled, expert nurse, had gradually intervened to assist Bessie in acknowledging her loss first in a cognitive sense: facing the fact that George was dead and Bessie would have to learn to live on her own. Then she worked with Bessie to realize that her whole life did not revolve around George or the current loss of him. This aspect of healing involved acquainting Bessie with her intuitive awareness. Finally, as Bessie integrated her loss of George with her increasing knowledge and appreciation of herself, she was open to a spiritual experience of transcendent awareness in which she could reconfirm her unity with the universe. Through the authentic relationship she experienced with Margaret, Bessie felt genuine healing.

FROM COGNITION TO TRANSCENDENCE

Human beings seek healing to restore connections with one another and to enjoy harmony within the universe. We seek healing as we try to make sense of our experiences and to establish meaning and purpose in living. To recognize our need for healing, we must first realize that we feel disconnected or out of synchrony with the world. This recognition and realization are the beginnings of awareness. This awareness is a cognitive experience: it consists of our knowledge about the material world and our physical bodies. Consciously knowing facts and processing the constant flow of information coming in through the senses is cognitive awareness. It is fundamental and common to all human beings. It is often brought fully to our attention through disease, injury, or malfunction of the body. Nurses respond to persons who are diseased or injured by assisting with the basic elements of daily care. The nurse, as well as the client, has cognitive awareness of the physical dimension of human experience.

Awareness occurs in other, more abstract ways as well. The other types of awareness, the intuitive and the transcendent types, are less familiar because we have not yet developed the language to communicate clearly about this type of awareness and because many persons well-trained in science and logic have placed little value on them. Intuitive awareness, as we have seen in earlier chapters, includes another way of knowing wherein facts or truths are known or felt directly rather than arrived at through a linear process of rational analysis. An intuitive flash experienced by a nurse or a client is an example of this type of awareness. It often leaves the person who experiences it with a sense of mystery or confusion because it is difficult, if not impossible, to put this type of awareness into words that others can understand. Moreover, it is difficult to find another person to share the awareness in the same way, thus calling into question the "reality" of such knowledge and experience. Nursing care given in highly complex environments where situations are changing rapidly, such as an intensive care unit, is ripe with opportunity for witnessing this type of awareness in nurse and client. Nurses who work in such a setting develop an expertise or wisdom based on incorporating small changes in the cues from their clients. Their intuitive awareness of these changes bypasses the usual slower, linear cognitive processes of rational thinking and they suddenly know that a client's status is changing and they respond automatically, without thinking specifically about what to do or how to do it. Likewise, many clients who are attuned to the inner functioning of their bodies express intuitive awareness about impending death or about unexpected recovery. Again, in the healing environment between nurse and client, intuitive awareness is evident.

Transcendent awareness is even more abstract. This awareness is found in experiences of intense tenderness and intimacy between people. Similar to the intuitive type of awareness, such direct knowing is also very personal and poorly understood by others. It differs from intuitive awareness because it is not bound by time or material/physical barriers to other forms of communication and patterns of knowing. It is the exchange of energy that occurs without rational thinking and analyzing, it is sudden like the intuitive, and it permits the closest and most intimate communication between beings. It is an awareness of a spiritual dimension of being human. By definition, transcendent means to go beyond the ordinary. Thus, transcendent awareness goes beyond the usual attention to the physical dimension of the world.

In describing phases of intervention for persons with hypertension, Thomas (1989) addresses the three types of awareness presented here. Her intervention is called transactional psychophysiological (TP) therapy and involves computer-assisted monitoring of blood pressure and heart rate during therapeutic communication. In the initial phase of the intervention, the client learns to observe herself. This phase focuses on the physiological processes and clients learn details of their heart and blood pressure with the assistance of cardiovascular monitoring devices. This phase promotes cognitive awareness. In the second phase of the intervention, the client learns to connect feelings with physiological response. Again, this process is facilitated by the feedback from the cardiovascular monitoring devices. This phase promotes intuitive awareness. In the final phase of the intervention, the client focuses on listening to the meaning of feelings and physiological responses within the body. The meaning of the individual's life and the capacity for developing inner peace are addressed. This phase promotes transcendent awareness. Although Thomas does not address these types of awareness directly, clearly the phases of the TP intervention promote each of the types of awareness discussed here.

In this book, each of these types of awareness is presented through an illustrative vignette. The intent of the vignettes and presentation of related concepts and theories is not to provide a taxonomy or cookbook approach to nursing practice. Rather, the intent is to appeal to the reader to include every dimension of human consciousness and intelligence in the relationship that promotes healing in persons. Human intelligence includes other dimensions beyond the cognitive, but the intuitive and transcendent dimensions have, until recently, received little attention in scientific circles. Awareness for healing does not take place only in the nursing client but in the nurse-healer as well. All dimensions of intelligence and awareness must be brought to bear on this important process of healing.

FUTURE AWARENESS

Although practicing nurses can readily identify examples of each of these types of awareness in themselves and their clients, much remains to be discovered or created, particularly with respect to the intuitive and transcendent types of awareness. The latter two are difficult to study because they are abstractions of human experience that cannot be observed or measured directly. Moreover, these types of awareness, and the part they play in the healing of individual persons, are highly subjective and thus difficult to categorize. It is far simpler to practice nursing and the art of healing by focusing only on the cognitive awareness of client and nurse. Current nursing education and practice demonstrate a plethora of interventions and procedures based on cognitive awareness. Such interventions are predictable in terms of their applications and outcomes. These play a substantial part in the healing of persons. As other dimensions of human consciousness and awareness are considered, however, the interventions associated with developing them become far more complex, far less predictable, and much more matters of faith and trust.

References

Thomas, S. A. (1989). Spirituality: An essential dimension in the treatment of hypertension. *Holistic Nursing Practice, 3* (3), 47–55.

Tower, V. B. (1987). *The process of intuition* (2nd ed.) Wheaton, IL: The Theosophical Publishing House.

EXERCISES
TO ENHANCE
AWARENESS

Practice, the path of mastery, exists only in the present. You can see it, hear it, smell it, feel it.

G. Leonard, 1991, p. 28

Jeevaka

The following legendary story about a medical student named Jeevaka from the Ayurvedic tradition of medicine illustrates the creative synthesis of nature in the healing process (Kartha, 1993). The story goes that Jeevaka presented himself to his faculty mentor, whose name was Aatreya, for his final examination in the school of medicine. Aatreya gathered his class before him and verbally directed the students to spend one week exploring the countryside around the medical school. They were instructed to return with samples of minerals, animals, plants, or any other substances they could find that *did not* have any medicinal or healing properties.

The next week was filled with anxious activity in the hills surrounding the medical school as the examinees frantically dug and scraped, pulled and squeezed, and amassed the evidence to present to their teacher. At the end of the week, the graduating physicians returned to Aatreya with a vast array of leaves, flowers, animal secretions, rocks, bones, and dirt. Only Jeevaka turned up with empty hands and pockets. His teacher asked him if he had decided not to take this final examination to which Jeevaka replied, "Dear teacher, I did as you instructed us to do. For as long as I have studied with you, I have searched for healing in the universe. At this time of my final examination, I went out and discovered as I have before that the entire universe is filled with healing power. There is no plant or animal, mineral or chemical that does not contain such power. The presence of healing is everywhere around us. I ask that you evaluate the results of my medical education on this response." Aatreya embraced Jeevaka and sent him on his way to practice the art of healing.

This chapter focuses on practice in enhancing awareness. Once the nurse-healer masters these exercises, they can then be used as creative interventions to facilitate the development of awareness in nursing clients. The first set of exercises concerns expanding awareness through sensory experiences. The second set of exercises involves creative activities that result in physical products to remind you of increasing awareness. The third set includes exercises to enrich awareness of inner strength and wisdom. Just as Jeevaka learned that all of the universe can be used for the process of healing, so individuals, clients and nurses, can learn through enhancing awareness that the power to heal is all around.

SENSORY AWARENESS

This set of exercises promotes awareness of physical sensations. The primary sensations of seeing, hearing, touching, smelling, and tasting bring much more information about the world into our minds and bodies than we are generally conscious of. Expanding awareness of the variety of sensations experienced may contribute to the healing process.

How Much Do I See?

Practice looking at the items in figure 9.1 for a given number of seconds. Here is a picture of several simple objects. Spend 5 seconds looking at and concentrating on the picture, then cover the page and list the items you remember seeing. How did you do? How did your eyes feel while you looked at the picture? How did they feel as you tried to remember all the items in the picture?

Listening to Nature

Go alone to a quiet natural place such as a park, ocean, or lake. Close your eyes and just listen to the sounds. Attend separately to each new noise, such as the barking of a dog, the chirping of

FIGURE 9.1 *How much do I see?*

a bird, or the crashing of a wave. After identifying each sound, begin to listen to yourself. What do you hear? Is your mind chattering? Can you hear the rhythm of your breathing or your heart beating? Focus now on the harmonics of the noises within your mind-body and the sounds of the universe. Concentrate on synchronizing these rhythms. After returning home, write down your impressions of this experience.

Touch and Tell

Find a friend who is willing to do this exercise with you. Ask this person to fill a small paper bag with at least 10 small objects with different textures. For example, a piece of sandpaper, an eraser, and a rose petal all have very different textures. After your friend has assembled the objects in the bag, reach into the bag and without looking inside the bag, tell your friend what the objects feel like (e.g., smooth, cold, soft). Your first urge might be to identify the object (e.g., the eraser), but resist this urge and simply describe the sensation. Be aware of differences that you feel between your dominant and nondominant hand.

Sniff Safely in Solitude

This exercise is completely safe because it allows you to experience the odors of your own body when nobody else is around to watch you or evaluate your behavior. When you are alone and in the process of getting dressed in the morning or undressed at night, take a few minutes to sniff around your own body. Start with your fingernails, then work your way up your hands and arms. What different aromas are there? If you are agile enough, repeat the exercise with your toes, feet, and legs.

The Taste Test

At your next meal, simply concentrate on the variety of taste sensations you experience. Distinguish between sour, salty, sweet, and bitter. After the meal, write down the various taste sensations you experienced. As you recall them, what memories come to mind? For example, if you tasted something sour during the meal, reflect a few moments on what other things you have eaten that were sour and on memories that you associate with the taste of that particular food. For example, if you had sauerkraut at your meal, you might remember certain times in your childhood when you ate sauerkraut and the emotions that accompanied that experience.

Dimensions of Physical Reality

Close your eyes and imagine an orange. After exploring the orange as completely as you wish, open your eyes and write down everything you can remember about how you imagined the orange. After completing this list, get an orange and examine it in detail. How does it look? How does it feel to touch? How does it look when it is peeled, when the segments are separated? How does the inside of the peel feel different from the outside? How many different textures does the orange contain? Then take a bit of the orange. How does it taste? What sensations do you experience as you chew and swallow the orange? What new things did you learn about an orange from this exercise? What new things did you learn about yourself?

Ambidextrous Activities of Daily Living

Spend time doing your routine daily activities with each of your hands. For example, if you usually hold your drinking glass in your left hand, hold it in the right hand. If you routinely open the door with your right hand, let your left hand do it for a day. At the end of the day, ask yourself the following questions:

1. How do my hands feel?

2. Am I more aware of the importance of my hands?

3. Did I know that my nondominant hand was so useful and capable?

Colorful Sensations

Take a walk through a garden with flowers blooming in it and note the wide variety of colors: red, lavender, green, yellow, and pink. Concentrate on each color separately for a few seconds, then close your eyes. Now focus again on each color, one at a time, beginning with the red. Allow the color to become as rich and vibrant as you can possibly imagine. Tune in to all the shapes, smells, sounds, and bodily sensations that this color evokes. Slowly continue through each of the colors you have just seen until each has been thoroughly experienced. Then open your eyes and record your responses to the exercise in a notebook.

Colorful Drawings

Seat yourself comfortably at a table with several sheets of blank paper and a set of colored pencils or markers. Relax for a few moments and then without consciously thinking about the color, pick up a pencil and begin to draw on the paper. Don't force yourself to draw anything in particular. Simply watch your hand as it freely draws something colorful. Feel free to add other colors to the drawing as you sit quietly and enjoy the exercise. Later go back to the drawing and examine the colors you used. What do those colors mean? Are they bright and cheerful or dull and gloomy? What type of awareness does this evoke in you?

CREATIVE AWARENESS

This set of exercises focuses on enhancing awareness by creating objects that you can review and enjoy more than once. The point of the exercises is not to produce objects for others to review and evaluate. Rather, the aim is to produce tangible evidence of your experience that can act as a stimulus to continue in developing awareness of your infinite capacities.

Awareness Scrapbook

Use a three-ring binder (notebook) and begin collecting pictures from magazines, newspaper articles, or other objects that appeal to you. Include some blank pages for writing your reflections about these objects. Don't try to force the issue, but after collecting several things of interest, examine them carefully and identify a theme. You may find that these objects reflect an increasing awareness of suffering in the world (e.g., you collected pictures of children starving or articles about war-torn countries) or an increasing awareness of startling changes in technology (e.g., you collected articles about new computer programs or medical treatments). Write down your reflections about this theme. Continue this process until your awareness of this theme feels saturated.

Ambidextrous Again

The purpose of this exercise is to focus awareness on the tendency to allow one side of the brain and body to act dominant to the other. It is an adaptation of an activity proposed by Capacchione (1988) to discover talent that may be hidden. Materials needed include a large piece of blank paper and two felt-tip markers or a chalkboard and two pieces of chalk. With one writing instrument in each hand, draw a symmetrical design using both hands simultaneously. This should form a picture with one side as the mirror image of the other side. On a new sheet of paper or another section of the chalkboard, draw different spontaneous designs with both hands at the same time. After completing the drawings, stand back and ask yourself these questions:

1. How did it feel to make these drawings?

2. What do I like about what I see?

3. What do these drawings tell me about myself that I didn't know before?

The Illogical Meaning of Life

This exercise invites you to examine the meaning of your life through the use of a metaphor and is adapted from von Oech's (1990) treatise on creativity. Think about the meaning of your life and identify two types of metaphors for it. One type of metaphor deals with a game and the other can be of any category that you like. The main idea is to answer the question, "What is my life like?" and then draw or write about the metaphor. For example, in the first category, you may say, "My life is like a tennis ball constantly going up and down" or you may draw a picture of the ball bouncing off the court. One of von Oech's examples is "Life is like a banana. You start out green and get soft and mushy with age" (p. 50). Draw or write what your life is like.

Put Your Mother on the Ceiling

This exercise is patterned after a book of the same name by Richard de Mille (1981). It is a delightful exercise in imagination that illustrates how creative the mind can be. The exercise, and others like it in de Mille's book, is best played by two people and is appropriate for use with children. It is similar to more advanced exercises of guided imagery, which are beyond the scope of this book, and requires that the person exercising imagination be free of distractions and have a desire to play.

The person practicing this imagination game (subject) begins by closing his eyes and imagining a blank piece of paper on which he draws the room in which the exercise is taking place. The other person helping the subject to imagine his mother on the ceiling (guide) instructs the subject to do this drawing in imagination. When the subject indicates that this mental drawing is complete, the guide suggests that he puts a mother on the ceiling of the room. The guide proceeds then to suggest other places to put the mother: on the chair, in a corner, and so on. The guide then suggests that the subject change the color of the mother's hair several times, moving from possible colors such as brown and gray to imaginative colors such as purple with pink polka dots. The game continues as the guide suggests activities for the mother to do such as standing on one foot, hopping around a chair, or singing a song. The game concludes when the guide suggests that the mother go back to her own home and the subject is instructed to erase the piece of paper so there are no more pictures of the room, and then to open his eyes and look around at the real room.

Unusual Inventions

The purpose of this exercise is to help you become aware of creative possibilities for problem solving or enjoying life to its fullest. Take several objects from your desk or a drawer in your kitchen. Play around with them by putting them in unusual combinations. Then write a description of your new invention and identify a possible market for this.

Word-Picture Associations

This is a fun activity to do when you are really bored! It also can help to move you out of a position where you feel stuck or rigid. It is an adaptation of an association exercise suggested by Nadel, Haims, and Stempson (1990). Following is a list of words that seem very unrelated. Begin by drawing a schematic representation of each pair of words. Then make a list of all the concepts, concrete or abstract, that come to your mind about the association of these unusual word pairs.

flower-baseball   watermelon-zebra

jellybean-closet   secret-chair

dog-hammer   skate-window

INNER AWARENESS

This set of exercises synthesizes some of the previous types of awareness into the experience of unity within. These exercises may be more difficult to do at first. Remember that there is no right or wrong way to do them. Allow yourself the freedom to play with them and enjoy whatever feels good about them.

Mandala Meditation

Mandala is a Sanskrit word meaning circle (Jung, 1973). In Tibetan Buddhism, it is a ritual instrument whose purpose is to assist with meditation and concentration. There are several ways to do this exercise. First, identify an object nearby that is basically a circular design with a center (or you can use the mandala in figure 9.2). Seat yourself in a comfortable position and focus all of your attention on the center of the design for a few seconds. Then look away and think about what you felt and experienced. Next, draw a geometric circular design with a center and concentrate on it for a few seconds. Was the second experience similar to or different from the first one? Walk around your home and identify other mandalas (e.g., a light fixture, a doorknob, a plate, or a piece of jewelry). Repeat the exercise with each of these articles in the next few days. Are you aware of any calm feelings

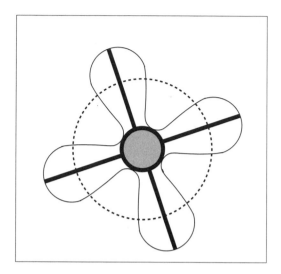

FIGURE 9.2   *Mandala: What does it symbolize to you?*

associated with this exercise? Do you tend to return to certain objects because of a comforting feeling associated with them?

Focus on Healing

Sit quietly and focus inwardly — do an assessment of the body, then focus on a part that is diseased or painful. Draw an outline of the body, then draw and color that part of the body. Use colors to express how that part of the body feels; e.g., temperature, texture. (This is like Sally in chapter 1 where she drew a picture of her scar.) Carry on an interview with the painful or diseased body part. Allow the body part to answer the interview questions by writing with the nondominant hand. The interview could contain the following types of questions:

1. Who are you?
2. How do you feel?
3. What caused you to feel this way?
4. What do you want from me?

Record any new insights you gain from the interview (Capacchione, 1988).

References

Capacchione, L. (1988). *The power of your other hand.* North Hollywood, CA: Newcastle Publishing Co., Inc.

de Mille, R. (1981). *Put your mother on the ceiling.* Santa Barbara: Ross-Erikson Publishers.

Jung, C. G. (1973). *Mandala symbolism.* Princeton: Princeton University Press.

Kartha, D. K. M. (1993). Jeevaka's test/Buddhist. *Parabola: The Magazine of Myth & Tradition, 18* (1), 82–83.

Leonard, G. (1991). The journey to mastery. *Noetic Sciences Review, 19,* 27–30.

Nadel, L., Haims, J., & Stempson, R. (1990). *Sixth sense: The whole-brain book of intuition, hunches, gut feelings, and their place in your everyday life.* New York: Prentice-Hall Press.

von Oech, R. (1990). *A whack on the side of the head: How you can be more creative.* New York: Warner Books.

Suggested Reading

Ferrucci, P. (1982). *What we may be.* Los Angeles: J. P. Tarcher, Inc.

Halpin, M. (1982). *Imagine that!* Dubuque, IA: Wm. C. Brown Company Publishers.

Morris, S. (1988). *The next book of omni games.* New York: New American Library.

Prather, H. (1981). *A book of games.* New York: Doubleday & Company, Inc.

Quereau, T., & Zimmermann, T. (1992). *The new game plan for recovery.* New York: Ballantine Books.

Simonton, O. C., & Henson, R. (1992). *The healing journey.* New York: Bantam Books.

Vaughan, F. (1986). *The inward arc.* Boston: New Science Library.

ANNOTATED
BIBLIOGRAPHY

Articles and books are abstracted below to provide a bird's-eye view of important literature used in the development of this book. The author encourages the readers of this book to pursue in full those references about which they wish to know more. Bibliographic entries are made according to major subject categories. These categories are awareness and consciousness, biological bases of consciousness, fuzzy logic, intuition, nursing theory and philosophy, healing phenomena, and ethics. They represent many of the topics that were addressed in previous chapters and include many new materials that have been published since this book was conceptualized. My hope is that the individual reader will be stimulated to explore the areas of interest to her.

Awareness and Consciousness

Chopra, D. (1991, Winter). Awareness: Maker of reality. *Noetic Sciences Review, 20,* 14–16.

Chopra is a physician trained in India and the United States. In this article, he describes the intimate relationship between mind and body. He gives examples of people who were born blind, then gained sight as surgeons removed their cataracts. These people had no experience with the meaning of sight. "The eye refuses to see what the mind does not know" (p. 14). Pure awareness is existing without form. Awareness is pure sensation, motionless silence contacted in meditation. Quantum physics shows that matter and energy have no objective, concrete existence. Reality is "everyone's personal creation . . . and . . . a spiritual experience is one in which pure awareness reveals itself as the maker of reality" (p. 16). Awareness is our source of creation. "Repeated experience of pure awareness allows this healing to take place" (p. 16). When all is in balance, human awareness lives in the absolute state of the self and the relative state of the self. "When awareness is completely balanced, communicating with the outside world is instantaneous and automatic. It happens with the touch of thought" (p. 16).

Mishlove, J. (1993). *The roots of consciousness.* Tulsa: Council Oak Books.

Jeffrey Mishlove provides a comprehensive survey of the philosophical and scientific exploration of consciousness. He covers the phenomena of dreams in the ancient world as well as the traditions of Greek and Hebrew religions. The folklore of consciousness is also explored in terms of astrology and out-of-body experiences. Current research findings about extrasensory perception, psychokinesis, and psionics are presented and he ends with various theoretical models of consciousness.

Poppel, E. (1988). *Mindworks: Time and conscious experience.* Boston: Harcourt Brace Javonovich, Publishers.

This book presents a fascinating model of human consciousness and awareness of time. Poppel conducted several experiments to track mental processes during reading, speaking, and other daily activities. The book contains interesting conclusions about the working of the unconscious mind and its relationship to such phenomena as dreams and poetry.

Biological Bases of Consciousness

Black, I. B. (1991). *Information in the brain: A molecular perspective.* Cambridge, MA: The MIT Press.

The purpose of this book is to examine how the mind works at a biological level. Black, who is a clinical neurologist, presents the cellular biology of information processing within the human nervous system. He discusses the function of hormones and neurotransmitters in the communication of information within the nervous system and includes many drawings and figures to illustrate main points. Many chapters are highly technical but each is well-organized with implications and conclusions about major hypotheses presented. Major theories and research findings are synthesized and the book contains a helpful glossary of technical terms.

Crick, F. (1994). *The astonishing hypothesis: The scientific search for the soul.* New York: Charles Scribner's Sons.
Crick, who is probably best known for his discovery with James Watson of the structure of DNA, presents a fascinating approach to understanding human consciousness and awareness. He begins with the concept of visual awareness and identifies the biological structures and functions of how the brain sees. He presents a compelling argument for the genetic and biochemical substrates of awareness and consciousness and provides many examples to test people's assumptions about the reality of what they see.

Gazzaniga, M. S. (1992). *Nature's mind: The biological roots of thinking, emotions, sexuality, language, and intelligence.* New York: Basic Books.
This book challenges the notion that the mind is a tabula rasa on which experience writes the words of knowledge. Rather, it focuses on the research supporting natural selection and suggests that knowledge is already implanted in the body. It contains a chapter on health care that concludes that even though selection theory dictates much of the way humans know and act, people can take personal control over their environments. The book ends with an epilogue about the nature of conscious experience, which he asserts is not learned and does not change throughout one's lifetime. The book is written by a neurobiologist who concludes that consciousness is a feeling which contributes to the human desire to survive and reproduce.

Ornstein, R. (1993). *The roots of the self: Unraveling the mystery of who we are.* New York: HarperCollins, Publishers.
In this book, Ornstein presents a very readable synthesis of major research findings about the biological basis of personality and temperament. He discusses how individuals respond to the stimuli from the external environment and how these responses are deeply rooted in biological structure. He adds that human beings have brains with a remarkable capacity for change and that the human race has barely begun to face the challenge of full development of this capacity.

Ornstein, R., & Swencionis, C. (Eds.). (1990). *The healing brain: A scientific reader.* New York: The Guilford Press.

This book provides a strong overview of current research concerning the relationship between the mind and the body. It includes chapters written by many of the leading researchers in such fields as medicine, psychology, and psychoneuroimmunology. It contains an excellent section on the concepts of stress and coping and ends with a call for more research to explore the relationship between consciousness and health.

Fuzzy Logic

Kosko, B. (1993). *Fuzzy thinking: The new science of fuzzy logic.* New York: Hyperion.

This is a book written by a philosopher and scientist who explains the basics of fuzzy theory as the gray area between black and white. Kosko shows how fuzzy logic imitates the functioning of the human brain in solving complex problems. He reviews many principles of philosophy that have shaped our perceptions and beliefs about what is true. He also addresses fuzzy sets as mathematical models of the real world and shows how these models apply to technology that more accurately represents the real world than the artificial technology of binary numbers. Finally, Kosko addresses the future and how human progress may be facilitated through further applications of fuzzy technology. He includes in this discussion of the future a provocative chapter on ethical questions raised by such applications.

McNeill, D., & Freiberger, P. (1993). *Fuzzy logic.* New York: Simon & Schuster.

McNeill and Freiberger trace the history of fuzzy logic from its invention by Lofti Zadeh at the University of California at Berkeley in 1964 through its current popularity in Japan to future applications throughout the world. The book is written in an interesting manner that does not focus on the technical aspects of the topic. It contains implications for health and healing through this fascinating application of computer technology.

Zadeh, L. A., & Kacprzyk, J. (Eds.). (1992). *Fuzzy logic for the management of uncertainty.* New York: John Wiley & Sons, Inc.

This book is an anthology of 32 technical papers on the subject of fuzzy logic. Edited by the founder of fuzzy logic, Lofti

Zadeh, and his colleague, Janusz Kacprzyk, the book contains a wide variety of presentations from the leading scientists in the area of fuzzy logic. The first part of the book contains a survey of approaches to approximate reasoning in the management of uncertainty. The next part is a discussion of fuzzy inference, knowledge representation, and implementation of methods in a knowledge-based system. The final part focuses on database systems using fuzzy theory. This book contains chapters written in a variety of different levels and is not for the faint-of-heart!

Intuition

Crandall, B., & Getchell-Reiter, K. (1993). Critical decision method: A technique for eliciting concrete assessment indicators from the intuition of NICU nurses. *Advances in Nursing Science, 16* (1), 42–51.

Crandall and Getchell-Reiter provide results of two research studies that support the use of the critical decision method for eliciting knowledge from expert nurses. They agree that expertise frequently results in a type of intuitive clinical judgment that is difficult for the expert to share with others because it is so familiar and difficult to communicate. The critical decision method assists the nurse in making intuitive knowledge more conscious and, therefore, more easily articulated to other less experienced nurses who can learn from those with expertise.

Nadel, L., Haims, J., & Stempson, R. (1990). *Sixth sense: The whole-brain book of intuition, hunches, gut feelings, and their place in your every day life.* New York: Prentice-Hall Press.

This is a layperson's book that summarizes interdisciplinary research about intuition as a powerful characteristic of the human mind. It contains useful material to enable the reader to identify personal intuitive skills and includes exercises to enhance these skills.

Parikh, J., Neubauer, F., & Lank, A. G. (1994). *Intuition: The new frontier of management.* Cambridge, MA: Blackwell Publishers.

Parikh, Neubauer, and Lank provide a fascinating discussion of intuition as both process and product. They define intuition as a skill, a personality trait, and as a predominant mode of being. They then place intuition within the context of business management and identify the ways in which it has been creatively employed around the world in making visions into realities.

Winter, T. (1988). *Intuitions: Seeing with the heart.* West Chester, PA: Whitford Press.

This is an interesting little book that is easy to read. In it, Winter, who is a psychologist, provides a glimpse into her personal encounters with trusting intuition in healing and in business. She describes several types of intuition, including the physical, emotional, and mental. The book contains meditations and several provocative exercises to improve awareness of intuition.

Nursing Theory and Philosophy

Johnson, J. L. (1991). Nursing science: Basic, applied, or practical? Implications for the art of nursing. *Advances in Nursing Science, 14* (1), 7–16.

Johnson asserts that the way nursing is viewed as a science is relevant to the art of nursing. She argues that nursing should be conceptualized as a practical science rather than as a basic or applied science. Knowledge in a practical science is developed to achieve particular objectives. Johnson provides definitions for each of these types of sciences and defines practical science as one that is applicable to performing specified tasks. She provides assumptions about the epistemology of nursing science. She further asserts that "nursing science must ultimately serve the art of nursing and not the reverse" (p. 9). She notes that in nursing practice, nurses apply scientific knowledge in addition to their own personal insights about the situation or tasks at hand. This reflects both the science and art of nursing.

Keegan, L. (1994). *The nurse as healer.* Albany, NY: Delmar Publishers, Inc.

In this book, Keegan poses and answers the question of how nurses become healers. She discusses the nature of healing and provides eight personal profiles of nurses who have been recognized for their healing behaviors. She provides a discussion of empowering the self for becoming a healer and includes many exercises to enhance one's awareness of healing potentials. She also traces the history of nurses as healers from the early Egyptians through contemporary holistic nurses. She ends with a chapter on recognizing the characteristics of self-actualized persons who may play an important part in healing.

Lamendola, F. P., & Newman, M. A. (1994). The paradox of HIV/AIDS as expanding consciousness. *Advances in Nursing Science, 16* (3), 13–21.

Based on Margaret Newman's theory of health as expanding consciousness, a naturalistic study was conducted with nine men who were either HIV-positive or had a diagnosis of AIDS. Findings were that these men experienced alienation during childhood, broke away from their families, and experienced loneliness as they searched for the meaning in their lives. The experience of HIV infection or AIDS was viewed as a turning point in their lives and resulted in their feeling more connected to others and more at ease with themselves. According to Newman's theory, consciousness is the total information about a person and is manifested in the pattern of interaction between the person and the environment. In this theory, disease is incorporated as a component of the pattern of interaction between the person and environment and, therefore, is subsumed within the concept of health.

Nagle, L. M., & Mitchell, G. J. (1991). Theoretic diversity: Evolving paradigmatic issues in research and practice. *Advances in Nursing Science, 14* (1), 17–25.

Nagle and Mitchell differentiate nursing science from nursing practice by stating that the former is the building of knowledge while the latter is the application of knowledge. They review the influence of logical positivism on the early development of nursing science and refer to it as the totality paradigm, which sees human beings as the sum of their biological, psychosocial, and spiritual components. In contrast, the simultaneity paradigm views human beings as greater than the sum of these components and sees reality as grounded within the context of a dynamic human-environment relationship. They cite Rosemarie Parse as the first nursing theorist to develop both a method for science and a method for nursing practice based on the simultaneity paradigm. These authors also argue for diversity in both nursing theory and practice.

Pohl, J. M., & Boyd C. J. (1993). Ageism within feminism. *IMAGE: Journal of Nursing Scholarship, 25,* 199–203.

These nursing authors recognize the increasing interest in feminist theory as a foundation for nursing science. They note, however, that aging women have not been included in the analysis of data based on a feminist framework. They present liberal, radical, and socialist feminist theories and identify how aging women are left out from each type of theory. Finally, they argue that feminist theory is appropriate for studying the health of aging women and has various implications for developing health policies. These policies are especially relevant in a time where long-term care is often in conflict with acute care with its emphasis on high technology.

Healing Phenomena

Cooper, D. M. (1990). Optimizing wound healing: A practice within nursing's domain. *Nursing Clinics of North America, 25* (1), 165–180.

Cooper states that the 1980s could be referred to as the era of the wound. Much that has been learned about healing and nursing is essential to that process. She notes, "Healing activities have always formed the basis of nursing practice" (p. 166). She discusses the observations of Myra Levine, a nurse theorist, who speaks of the nurse as the promoter of healing and the reintegration of wholeness. Levine recognized that because the nurse spends more time with patients than other health care professionals, nurses have the most influence on the healing process. Cooper adds, "Not unlike a waterfall, healing is a cascading process composed of multiple small goal-directed events that combine and result in the creation of something more complex and energy rich than any one component considered by itself. It is a process as intricate as any of the other major functions in the human body." (p. 170).

Cousins, N. (1989). *Head first, the biology of hope.* New York: E. P. Dutton.

This book by Norman Cousins contains an account of his ten years on the faculty of UCLA Medical School. Well-known for his book, *Anatomy of an Illness,* on the importance of humor in self-healing, Cousins left his position as editor of *Saturday Review* to work with medical educators, students, and researchers to explore how attitudes and other psychosocial variables influence healing in persons. He discusses the role of the brain and mind on disease and healing. He also reiterates that humans are innately equipped with resources for healing that are best enhanced by human relationships and interpersonal communication.

Duff, K. (1993). *The alchemy of illness.* New York: Pantheon Books.

This book is a personal account of the experiences of a woman suffering from chronic fatigue and immune dysfunction syndrome (CFIDS). The chapters are based on notes Kat Duff kept during her illness. She challenges traditional beliefs about health and illness and describes disease as a manifestation of healing. She chose the analogy of medieval alchemy to explore illness and healing as a spiritual transformation and traces her recovery through a growing awareness of her spiritual self.

O'Regan, B., & Hirshberg, C. (1993). *Spontaneous remission: An annotated bibliography.* Sausalito, CA: Institute of Noetic Sciences.

This recent volume documents 1385 different articles published on the spontaneous remission of cancer and other diseases. It includes abstracts and case histories from publications in various disciplines such as psychology and medicine. The authors note that there is no known epidemiology of remission because it is difficult to study. Cases are often seen after recovery with little empirical evidence to track. However, they trace the concept of spontaneous remission in the history of medical literature and suggest possible biological mechanisms based on immunological factors. They also draw attention to the role of the mind in this phenomenon and cite recent evidence in remission of cancer and AIDS.

Siegel, B. S. (1993). *How to live between office visits.* New York: HarperCollins Publishers.

In his latest book, Bernie Siegel, surgeon and author of *Love, Medicine & Miracles* and *Peace, Love & Healing,* provides an easy-to-read guide for practical ways to think about living and healing. One chapter is a do-it-yourself kit for healing and includes a discussion about the importance of finding a health professional with whom one can have a relationship. Another chapter focuses on the role of spiritual beliefs and practices in healing.

Ethics

Liaschenko, J. (1993). Feminist ethics and cultural ethos: Revisiting a nursing debate. *Advances in Nursing Science, 15* (4), 71–81.

In this article, Liaschenko re-examines nursing ethics from a feminist perspective. She begins by defining feminist ethics as characterized by acknowledging the oppression and domination of women. She then discusses and critiques the major school of thought in nursing ethics. She asserts that nursing practice exists within the context of social and institutional living and that nursing needs a feminist ethic. Such an ethic would address modes of resisting oppressive social and institutional conditions.

I N D E X

INDEX OF AUTHORS

Dear Parents:

Congratulations! Your child is taking the first steps on an exciting journey. The destination? Independent reading!

STEP INTO READING® will help your child get there. The program offers five steps to reading success. Each step includes fun stories and colorful art or photographs. In addition to original fiction and books with favorite characters, there are Step into Reading Non-Fiction Readers, Phonics Readers and Boxed Sets, Sticker Readers, and Comic Readers—a complete literacy program with something to interest every child.

Learning to Read, Step by Step!

Ready to Read   Preschool–Kindergarten
• big type and easy words • rhyme and rhythm • picture clues
For children who know the alphabet and are eager to begin reading.

Reading with Help   Preschool–Grade 1
• basic vocabulary • short sentences • simple stories
For children who recognize familiar words and sound out new words with help.

Reading on Your Own   Grades 1–3
• engaging characters • easy-to-follow plots • popular topics
For children who are ready to read on their own.

Reading Paragraphs   Grades 2–3
• challenging vocabulary • short paragraphs • exciting stories
For newly independent readers who read simple sentences with confidence.

Ready for Chapters   Grades 2–4
• chapters • longer paragraphs • full-color art
For children who want to take the plunge into chapter books but still like colorful pictures.

STEP INTO READING® is designed to give every child a successful reading experience. The grade levels are only guides; children will progress through the steps at their own speed, developing confidence in their reading. The F&P Text Level on the back cover serves as another tool to help you choose the right book for your child.

Remember, a lifetime love of reading starts with a single step!

Step into Reading, Random House, and the Random House colophon are registered trademarks of Penguin Random House LLC.

Visit us on the Web!
Seussville.com
StepIntoReading.com
randomhousekids.com

Educators and librarians, for a variety of teaching tools, visit us at RHTeachersLibrarians.com

Library of Congress Cataloging-in-Publication Data
Names: Rabe, Tish, author. | Brannon, Tom, illustrator.
Title: Cooking with the Grinch / by Tish Rabe ; illustrations by Tom Brannon.
Description: First edition. | New York : Random House, [2017] | Series: Step into reading.
Step 1 | Summary: The Grinch and Cindy Lou Who bake a Christmas surprise.
Identifiers: LCCN 2016034550 | ISBN 978-1-5247-1462-8 (trade pbk.) |
ISBN 978-1-5247-1463-5 (lib. bdg.)
Subjects: | CYAC: Stories in rhyme. | Baking—Fiction. | Christmas—Fiction.
Classification: LCC PZ8.3.R1145 Co 2017 | DDC [E]—dc23

Printed in the United States of America

10 9 8 7 6

This book has been officially leveled by using the F&P Text Level Gradient™ Leveling System.